Idyllic No More

Pacific Island Climate, Corruption, and Development Dilemmas

Pearl farming in Namdrik Atoll in the Marshall Islands, one of a few remote islands in the country engaged in locally-run sustainable development programs. Photo: Mattlan Zackhras.

Giff Johnson

ISBN: 978-1512235586; ISBN: 151223558X

The essays in this book were originally prepared as blogs for the Pacific Institute for Public Policy, www.pacificpolicy.org/, between 2013 and 2015. They have been edited for this publication.

Other books by Giff Johnson

• **Don't Ever Whisper: Darlene Keju — Pacific Health Pioneer, Champion for Nuclear Survivors**, 2013. www.donteverwhisper.com.

• **Nuclear Past, Unclear Future**, 2009. www.marshallislandsjournal.com.

To learn more about nuclear testing in the Marshall Islands, see Giff Johnson's Marshall Islands Nuclear News on Facebook.

Cover design: Benjie Digno, II.

Cover/back cover photos: Suzanne Chutaro, Ben Chutaro, Giff Johnson.

To all of the dedicated non-government organizations in the Pacific islands that are working on sustainable development programs and delivering critically needed community services: Keep walking the talk.

Out-of-school Marshallese youth in the Waan Aelon in Majel (Canoes of the Marshall Islands) program in Majuro learn vocational and life skills in a six-month training program that emphasizes outrigger canoe building and sailing, handicraft making, and cultural and academic learning. Photo: Isaac Marty.

Aerial view of the main island of Jabor in Jaluit Atoll, which hosts one of two public high schools that are located on remote atolls in the Marshall Islands.

Table of Contents

Preface

Out-migration from remote Pacific islands of people skilled in self-reliance and subsistence living is undermining hopes of a sustainable future.

In the late 1980s, while I was in Pohnpei interviewing people for stories about the then-relatively new Federated States of Micronesia, I had the good fortune to connect with former Yap Governor John Mangefel, who was then the FSM's national planner during the presidency of John Haglelgam.

After the usual preliminaries between a visiting reporter and a seasoned political figure, Mangefel offered a blunt evaluation of development progress in his nation. This was only a handful of years into the FSM's first Compact of Free Association funding package with the United States and a period when producing five-year national development plans was the routine. "Western-style economic development won't work in the FSM," Mangefel told me as we sat in his office in Palikir, the seat of the FSM government in Pohnpei. "Why not?" was the obvious response. "It's simple," Mangefel said. "In the FSM, if you work, you eat. If you don't work, you still eat." His point was, of course, that there was little incentive for the 40-hour workweek ethic required by government planners to advance "economic development" when local folks could eat at their uncle's house anytime they wanted.

Although Mangefel was the national planner, in essence he was telling me that the lofty economic goals spelled out in the government's five-year development plans wouldn't be realized, not as written, not as carried out, for the fact that these paper documents had little relationship to the "lifestyle" in the FSM, which mirrored how people lived in most islands in the region. Nevertheless, most people in government offices nominally charged with carrying out these development plans went through the motions of implementing western-style programs funded by donors, rarely offering as candid a view as the late Yap governor or attempting to reshape obviously unworkable plans. While island culture is often at odds with objectives laid out in modern planning, newer developments have added to the challenge of creating sustainable development or, even, delivery of essential health and education services.

Mangefel's comment was 25 years ago. In the interim, a culture of overseas travel has engaged government workers, supported and funded largely by donors, that keeps many managers of government services away from their homes four — or more — months of the year. Needless to say, if you're not at home, you're not delivering a service or implementing development initiatives.

As the world and the Pacific prepare to embark in 2015 on a new 15-year regime of "Sustainable Development Goals" (SDGs), we need look no further than the record of ineffective implementation of the "Millennium Development Goals" (MDGs) from 2000 to 2015. Ten of the 14 independent Pacific nations were unable to achieve a majority of the seven MDGs, and three failed to successfully implement a single one. So now the islands are signing up to implement 17 "Sustainable Development Goals." This would be almost laughable were poverty and lack of opportunities not a pervasive fact in urban centers around the Pacific, exacerbating income inequality and causing a downward spiral in people's quality of life.

And who, exactly, is going to implement government-approved strategic development plans? In my experience, it is a rare government worker who can avoid the offers of frequent international travel to stay at home and deliver work on the ground where it counts. In fact, the culture of travel and a general lack of engagement in creating a vision for national development has led to another, relatively new, phenomenon: that of handing the job of goal-setting and strategic planning to off-shore consultants who drop in for a few weeks at a time. For the most part, any plan that is not crafted by a range of the local citizenry, so-called "stakeholders" at all levels of society, has no buy-in and even less chance of success. In fact, a classic example of how even locally-produced reports and recommendations are relegated to the waste basket was the Comprehensive Adjustment Program produced by local experts in the Marshall Islands under mandate of the president a few years ago. If government ignored recommendations of its own Comprehensive Adjustment Program task force, a largely homegrown effort, what level of implementation will result from strategies produced by non-resident experts?

Widespread corruption and lack of accountability in governments in the Pacific is another factor obstructing sustainable development goals and delivery of services.

These are challenges that face virtually every government and island group in the Pacific, be they independent or territory. The FSM, Marshall Islands and Palau have one additional development challenge unique to their relationship with the United States. By virtue of the Compact of Free Association, citizens of these nations have visa-free access to the United States to live, work and study. As island economies stagnate and lack of job and educational opportunities predominate, principally in the FSM and Marshall Islands, thousands of islanders are voting with their feet by transplanting themselves to U.S. states and territories. Various estimates suggest the number of FSM and Marshall Islands citizens living in the U.S. is between 30 and 40 percent of the total populations. There is clearly a brain drain happening, particularly as islanders increasingly vacate remote outlying islands for the convenience first of urban centers and later for the U.S. But this is not necessarily a brain drain in the classic sense of western educated islanders seeking greener pastures. Yet this out-migration from the remote islands of people skilled in self-reliance and subsistence living is undermining hopes of a sustainable future because the only places in most Pacific islands that are self-sufficient to a high degree are the outer islands and rural villages — certainly not urban centers. Depopulate the villages and outer islands and what chance do islands have of implementing new Sustainable Development Goals?

If governments and donors that control the purse strings and access to technical assistance don't start reinventing their development agendas and means of implementation, in 15 years' time, we will again be lamenting the inability of our islands to make progress on the 17 Sustainable Development Goals being adopted as the framework for global development.

It is my hope that the following chapters offer some useful discussion of trends and challenges for people interested in engaging in key issues of the day facing Pacific islands.

Chapter One: Corruption Undermines Development Goals

Increasingly crowded urban centers in the Pacific islands face numerous challenges, including access to basic services such as education, healthcare and clean water. Photo: Ben Chutaro.

Corruption impacts development progress

'The commission of inquiry found that a nexus of prominent officials, lawyers and others, stole $300 million by inventing claims for compensation from the government, which highly placed members of the conspiracy then paid out.'

It is my observation that in 2014 there are more investigations into corruption being conducted in various parts of the Pacific. Why is this happening? Do citizens care more? Are the media and non-government groups like Transparency International and others exposing more wrongdoing? Are younger, overseas-educated islanders standing up for ethics in government? Are some government elected leaders, civil servants or private citizens blowing the whistle?

Where we see corruption reports spilling into the press, such as in Papua New Guinea and in the Marshall Islands, it is often because the situation has become so obvious and destructive, people at lower echelons are coming forward to provide evidence that gives law enforcement officials a foundation for successful investigations. Despite allegations and investigations, however, often few prosecutions are mounted and fewer people still end up paying a penalty. There are, of course, many reasons for this. Bottom line, however, is that in the Pacific, corruption generally pays with few consequences to the people involved — but the consequences to the country are many and serious: lack of public service in government offices and an inability to meet development, health and education goals.

In the Marshall Islands, investigations in late 2010 and 2011 into theft of United States grants to the Ministry of Health resulted in a series of successful prosecutions of low-to-mid-level Ministry of Health and Ministry of Finance staff. The scam involved using fake invoices to generate government purchase orders and checks that were cashed and distributed among the co-conspirators. No goods or services were received by the Ministry for the hundreds of thousands of dollars that was stolen. But an underlying problem was never addressed in these investigations: bid (tender) fraud. This was so even though Deloitte audits have shown multiple violations of the government procurement law over many years.

The depth of the problem became evident when the FY2010 audit was issued. It showed, for example, "potentially altered purchase requisitions, potentially altered price quotations, missing grant files/disbursement files, payments for goods that have been represented as not being received, and payments for services that have been represented as not being performed" for $1,621,565 of government spending. The Marshall Islands Journal in its September 30, 2011 edition headlined a two-page spread on this audit of government operations: "How much money was stolen in 2010?"

Fast-forward to January 2014, and eight government workers, including seven at the Ministry of Health, have been put on leave as a major investigation by the Auditor General and police continues piling up evidence that is expected to result in a series of prosecutions. The corruption issue surrounds allegations that a local company bribed government employees to win bids for hospital equipment and supply contracts.*

Despite the investigations in 2011 and 2014 showing theft and fraudulent use of large chunks of U.S. funding for health services, the U.S. government has not taken any specific action on what is being shown as a long-term, ingrained corruption problem — although the U.S. Government Accountability Office issued a recent report on U.S. funding to the Marshall Islands and Federated States of Micronesia calling on the U.S. Interior Department to strengthen oversight of grants.

In contrast, Australia appears to be taking a tougher line on its approximately A$500 million a year aid program to Papua New Guinea. Australian Foreign Minister Julie Bishop singled out PNG as a particularly poor performer as an aid recipient. "I find it distressing to know that despite the fact that Australia invests about half a billion dollars every year into Papua New Guinea, it will not meet one of its Millennium Development Goals (MDGs) — in fact it is going backwards," said Bishop in early 2014.

Australia cut $38 million from PNG because of corrupt practices in the tendering process for hospital medical kits. After a three-year delay, in December 2013, the PNG Supreme Court approved publication of an 812-page commission of inquiry into false compensation scams that cost the country more than $300 million. "This move, following other recent events, points to a possible turning of the tide against one of PNG's most pervasive problems, with the country ranked 150th by Transparency International out of 176 countries on its corruption index last year," wrote The Australian after the court overturned an injunction that had prevented publication in PNG of this extensive corruption inquiry. "The commission of inquiry found that a nexus of prominent officials, lawyers and others, stole $300 million by inventing claims for compensation from the government, which highly placed members of the conspiracy then paid out. The report recommends the criminal prosecution of 57 prominent people, many still in top positions."

The fact that people in government and connected to government in the two countries mentioned here have been able to engage in corrupt practices for many years demonstrates the challenge to bringing greater transparency and accountability to government operations. No doubt, there are similar practices evident in many other island nations.

There are people in governments around the region who see "government money" or aid funds from other nations as simply a pot of money waiting for anyone who is smart to get their hands on it. This is especially so in relation to donor funding. People bent on manipulating government finance systems for their own benefit — as demonstrated by the PNG commission of inquiry report and the most recent hospital bid fraud investigation in the Marshall Islands — outnumber the people attempting to enforce accountability and rule of law.

It goes far beyond thievery. Political level leaders and personnel in government ministries and agencies are responsible to deliver performance on MDGs, development plans, and a host of other government services. When large numbers are engaged in fraud, the results show not only in loss of money but in lack of performance. In early 2014, Marshall Islands President Christopher Loeak complained in a parliament session about the lack of service in government offices.

A review of progress among the 14 independent Pacific nations in meeting MDGs shows that PNG is not on track to meet a single one, while the Marshall Islands is on track on only two of seven. While a handful of countries are showing good MDG progress (Cook Islands and Niue, for example, are on track to meet all seven goals, and Palau is meeting six of seven), the average for the independent nations in the region is less than three out of the seven MDGs.

Every dollar that some government officials put in their pockets for personal use is a dollar not available for government services or supplies. Every hour spent hatching and implementing corrupt schemes (or even just showing up to work late and leaving early) is time not spent on public service. If government officials engaged in these practices, or turning a blind eye to them, think the results of corrupt practices are not evident, they are wrong: it is increasingly obvious, both from development performance reports and investigations into alleged wrongdoing as well as day-to-day problems island residents encounter when dealing with government offices, how corruption undermines national development progress.

* The manager of the pharmaceutical company Genesis pleaded guilty to a series of criminal charges in 2014 as part of a plea bargain agreement, and late in the year, the company agreed to pay a $400,000 fine and was banned from doing business in the Marshall Islands for ten years.

Corruption comes in many flavors

A performance audit of the tax auditing office within the Ministry of Finance showed that in 2010, 25 audits of local companies were planned but the sum total of none were conducted.

When media reports on government "corruption," it usually focuses on theft of money from government ministries or agencies. There is quite a bit of this across the Pacific, from Papua New Guinea to the Marshall Islands.

But more subtle practices of government both at high levels — not passing legislation that would improve the accountability environment — and at lower levels — losing grant money needed to provide public services by not filing timely reports with donors — are not often in view, but greatly impact operations of government.

To give a few examples from the Marshall Islands:

• Soon after taking office in 2011, Marshall Islands Auditor General Junior Patrick laid out a plan to expand audits to focus not only on finances, but performance of government offices. The expansion called for a near doubling of staff, more supervisory auditors, and ramped up fraud prevention work. But successive governments have failed to give his office the funds needed to hire all the staff his plan envisioned — despite confirmation of major theft of donor grant funds at the Ministry of Health in the 2010-to-2014 period.

• Legislation to replace the existing government ethics law with a stronger version, including requiring annual financial disclosure by high-level leaders, was introduced in 2012 and went nowhere. Admittedly it was introduced by opposition senators, which obviously reduces the chances of passage. But if our standard for evaluating this legislation is not political but rather whether or not it will improve accountability, then clearly, as the Auditor General spelled out in his testimony in support of the legislation, the Nitijela (parliament) missed another opportunity to improve government accountability and reduce corrupt practices.

• In October 2014, the Marshall Islands Journal reported on its front page that the U.S. government had, for the first time in 30 years, refused to fund the Ministry of Health's Family Planning program "due to the failure by the Marshall Islands to submit necessary documents in a timely fashion as well as the fact they did not demonstrate financial need." We might politely ask how the Ministry of Health in a country that has the Pacific's highest teen pregnancy rate could not "submit necessary documents" or "demonstrate financial need" to get routinely provided annual funding support from the U.S. federal government. In spite of this situation, employees still get their usual salaries.

• Both the Ministries of Health and Education routinely do not spend hundreds of thousands of dollars annually of budgeted, available money under the Compact of Free Association treaty with the U.S. Meanwhile, vendors providing services to these ministries often get paid late or not at all, and schools complain about lack of supplies and the hospital in Majuro routinely runs out of basic medicines.

• A recent performance audit of the tax auditing office within the Ministry of Finance, for example, showed that in 2010, 25 audits of local companies were planned but the sum total of none were conducted, while in 2011, 30 were planned and only eight carried out.

Omissions — not doing work that undermines public services, not passing legislation that would help anti-corruption enforcement — don't get the attention devoted to large-scale theft of government funds, but when all the omissions are added up, the price tag is hefty. This is why the Marshall Islands Auditor General's effort — and those of other Public Auditors in the region — to expand performance auditing is so important. Financial audits only tell us if paper work is in place to justify spending. Performance audits tell us what government offices are doing with their funds and if they are meeting their public service objectives. What our leaders and public servants are doing when they are in their offices (we hope) 40 hours each week is an important question for audits — and the public — to ask.

Corruption comes in many forms: coming late and leaving early but getting fulltime pay, not carrying out the mission of a government office, manipulating tenders and funds for personal interest, and seeing some or all of the above and doing nothing about it. As we've seen in big nations such as the United States that have a significant level of audit and enforcement capability that does not exist in most small islands, corruption can still be widespread. Because it's not readily observable in our islands does not mean it doesn't exist. Let's start looking and resolving corruption problems as we find them so the public gets the benefit of the "public service."

Chapter Two: Development Dilemmas and Opportunities

Development initiatives for remote islands and rural villages dwindle as people migrate to the urban centers and, from the freely associated states to the United States, in ever larger numbers. A few initiatives run by local governments in the Marshall Islands — such as pearl farming and virgin coconut oil processing in Namdrik, and fish farming in Majuro — stand out as developments that are potentially sustainable, and are generating jobs and revenue for the nation. Photo: Mattlan Zackhras.

Poverty and societal breakdown go hand-in-hand

'Cash infusions for budgetary support, provide by the World Bank and ADB, have, contrary to sensible intentions, enabled the Marshall Islands to continue the current policy regime without need for adjustment.'

When videos of a toddler in the Marshall Islands smoking a cigarette and drinking from a can of beer were posted to Facebook in 2013, it caused outrage and concern among many local residents. The smoking baby incident, like a number of other recent heartbreaking "firsts" — including a young mother tossing her baby into a garbage dumpster in Majuro — is a bellwether related to social and economic conditions in the country.

"We have so many neglected children," said a high-level government official after the incident with the smoking baby was exposed. There is no doubting this observation when child malnutrition, school truancy levels, and high school dropout rates are considered. Many appear to think that it is the responsibility of one ministry or another or a non-government service provider to respond to this type of situation. This misses the point that a growing problem of this nature requires a whole of government approach, with policy focus rather than a band-aid response from one agency.

The deeper issue for the Marshall Islands is the breakdown of traditional family systems, a breakdown that is accelerating because of migration from remote outer islands to the urban centers and the urban poverty that is deepening each year. Many political leaders who are in a position to respond by directing resources and policy focus to social and poverty concerns tend to ignore or discount the issue. A not insignificant number take the view that poverty is not a serious problem in the Marshall Islands.

The problem of increasing poverty was first exposed in a 2004 report that provided a snapshot look at one urban neighborhood in Majuro. This study, which became know as the 'Jenrok Report,' described the daily challenge of life for Marshall Islanders in this area of the capital atoll: "People in Jenrok do not have access to clean and drinkable water," only half of the homes were connected to the city water system, many rely on ground wells that Environmental Protection Authority testing shows are "severely contaminated," and "overcrowded living conditions in Jenrok have led to unhealthy and unsafe environments."

The same could have been said about other sections of Majuro and Ebeye, the other urban center in the Marshalls. The issuance of this report sparked little government response, other than the provision of donor-provided water catchment tanks to households a few years later and a short-lived recycling project.

Two years later, the Asian Development Bank funded a social and economic report on the country that was titled 'Juumemmej' (Stand Awake). The title is a navigator's term, describing the responsibility of the navigator or captain to guide his canoe for the safety of the passengers, and it was employed to gain attention of leaders to pressing community and economic issues facing the nation. It also zeroed in on increasing poverty and the impact this was having on the country as well as the stimulus for out-migration to the United States. The report was criticized by some political leaders for being off base. While it was obvious the criticism, not the report, was missing the point, at least the public debate over the report raised some awareness about poverty and hardship. In fact, many people in a community that the 1999 census said was experiencing a 30 percent unemployment rate (double that for youth) understand poverty all too clearly.

Despite poverty taking hold over the past two decades, members of parliament rarely talk about the need to create jobs or address poverty reduction. Donors, of course, do talk about poverty reduction and occasional workshops address it. But there has been little government policy or budget response to this looming issue that is driving other problems. Indeed, the slow progress on meeting Millennium Development Goals — the Marshall Islands is only 'on-track' on two of the eight goals, and the lack of progress on the first MDG, alleviating poverty — tells the story.

A Graduate School USA economic report for fiscal year 2012 included commentary about growing poverty in the country. "While abject poverty, starvation and destitution are not yet present in the RMI, there are clear signs that certain groups are facing increasing hardship. The Marshall Islands is demonstrating mixed progress on MDG One (eradicate extreme poverty and hunger), and there are growing concerns over high unemployment, financial hardship (including declining real incomes coupled with large consumer debt), hunger and poor nutrition," the report said.

Despite this, there has been little change in budget policy and many proposed government reforms have stagnated. The Graduate School USA report observed: "While there is no doubt that the refinancing of the Marshalls Energy Company debt was a beneficial move, the fiscal targets of the Asian Development Bank loan were not achieved. The Comprehensive Adjustment Program has failed to gain any momentum. In addition, tax reform has remained under consideration for several years, and the outcome remains uncertain. Similarly, both the state owned enterprises and external debt legislation appear to be on the backburner...Recent cash infusions for budgetary support, provide by the World Bank and ADB, have, contrary to sensible intentions, enabled the Marshall Islands to continue the current policy regime without need for adjustment."

Is this what Marshall Islanders want? No one knows because there has not been a national consultation to set development objectives in more than a decade. And the nature of the culture tends to prevent overt questioning or criticism of decision makers. Instead, Marshall Islanders have voted with their feet, with out-migration to the United States averaging 1.5 percent of the population annually over the past 10 years. An estimated one-third of all Marshall Islanders now reside in the United States.

Still, a key point for the country is that money is not the primary problem for addressing poverty and development needs. Resources are available (in fact, virtually every year, the ministries of Education and Health do not spend all of the funding they receive from the U.S. government). The critical challenge has been political will to reform the government's policy framework to address the changing economic environment in the country, and the management and performance of the government sector, which drives the economy.

It seems unlikely that this will change in the immediate future. In the meantime, the outflow of Marshall Islanders to the United States is expected to continue as people seek a brighter future for their families.

What is the future of remote island populations?

Continued migration away from the outer islands is undermining goals and values national governments claim to endorse.

The needs and interests — indeed the very future of — remote populations in the region are often lost in economic development models promoted by urban center politicians, government managers, development planners and donor partners. While there is a lot of ink expended in reports concerning the need for "sustainable development" or for the promotion of "self-reliance" in Pacific islands, little attention gets paid to remote islands and villages. It's a paradox of the Pacific that while development planners tout economic and other policies purportedly aimed at increasing self-reliance and sustainability, day-to-day policies tend to undermine life in the only location where people are, in fact, mostly self-reliant: the outer islands and remote villages.

As life gets more difficult in these remote island areas, increasingly people are voting with their feet by migrating to the urban centers, increasing pressure on already over-burdened government health, education and social services, or where they can, hopping on a plane to the United States, New Zealand or Australia.

The gap between government policy and goals for sustainable development and actual results needs to be a focus of discussions around the region.

The Marshall Islands may be an extreme example of this, but offers much food for thought. The 2011 national census report shows the population declined significantly on the outer islands, with all but three outer islands seeing a drop in numbers from the last census in 1999. Eighteen outer islands experienced population decreases, as people moved to Majuro, Ebeye or the United States. Today there are 4,000 fewer people on remote islands — about seven percent of the total population having left the outer islands between 1999 and 2011.

This migration has produced a major population shift. The census shows that almost three-quarters of all Marshallese in the Marshall Islands now live in Majuro and Ebeye. In the 1960s, more people lived on outer islands than in the two urban centers. Obviously, there is a continuing flow of people heading to the U.S. looking for jobs and educational opportunities, or medical care they cannot get in the Marshall Islands, and with the visa-free entry status that Marshallese, Micronesians and Palauans enjoy, moving to the U.S. is a relatively easy option.

The change in outer islands-urban population numbers carries an underlying message: as life gets more difficult on the remote islands, people move for better opportunities. The big picture question for leaders is: What is the overriding goal for the outer islands? Do we want people living there 20 years from now? If the answer is "yes," then there are many development issues and needs that should be addressed. If the answer is "no," then continuing on the path the country is on will quite likely produce the result of emptying the outer islands.

Ironically, the Compact of Free Association between the U.S. and the Marshall Islands, Federated States of Micronesia and Palau lists goals of "self-sufficiency" through economic development. The first Compact, which went into effect in 1986, affirms "the interest of the Government of the United States in promoting the economic advancement and self-sufficiency of the peoples of the Trust Territory of the Pacific Islands." Compact II, which replaced the first Compact in 2004, states: "The Government of the United States reaffirms its continuing interest in promoting the economic advancement and budgetary self-reliance of the people of the Republic of the Marshall Islands."

This is all well and good, but in light of the exodus from the outer islands, either something is wrong with implementation of development programs or it could simply be that now, with two generations of islanders born in the urban centers, the ties of government managers to the outer islands are becoming more and more tenuous. Many local officials may simply not realize the importance of improving the quality of life on the outer islands to the entire nation.

Outer islands "development" needs are more than just the arrival of a cargo and passenger vessel every few months or occasional airline service, though these are critical to quality of life. The emphasis donors place on "developing the private sector" and promoting "good governance" generally translates into funding, focus, training and other efforts in the urban centers.

Still, the fact is, the only place in Marshall Islands and many countries in the region where "self-reliance" is apparent is on the outer islands or remote villages. Continued migration away from the outer islands and lack of any big picture plan to increase their attractiveness and therefore maintain or increase the population base — is undermining goals and values national governments claim to endorse.

There are some exceptions to the rule. One is Namdrik Atoll, where an energetic team of Mayor Clarence Luther and Senator Mattlan Zackhras has produced a high degree of economic activity, including a pearl oyster farm, virgin coconut oil processing and coconut tree replanting. This resulted in the atoll gaining United Nations Development Program recognition with the Equator Prize in 2012 — Namdrik was one of only three islands in the Pacific to receive recognition from UNDP's global sustainable development competition.

The local government at Utrik, an atoll in the north that suffers regular fresh water shortages for lack of rain, acted on the problem in 2010 by installing solar and wind-powered reverse osmosis water making equipment that produces over 3,000 gallons of potable water daily. Locals were trained to operate and maintain the unit, and it remains a functional and integral part of the island. In contrast, national government programs for years have been focused on providing catchment tanks to other islands, which is useful when it's raining. But a tank doesn't help when there is no rain for months. The severe drought in the northern islands in the Marshalls during 2013 prompted aid agencies to spend millions of dollars providing water, food, and small reverse osmosis units for emergency water service to over 15 outer islands. The provision of small, 300-to-400 gallon per day water makers was a stopgap measure that provided some relief. Unlike the Utrik system, however, it was not sustainable because these small units depended on Majuro-based technicians to service them. It would seem logical that the government and its aid partners would look at the Utrik model as a way to sustainably manage drought conditions, and improving health and quality of life on other islands.

In the 1990s, the NGO Youth to Youth in Health engaged about 20 percent of the inhabited outer island communities in a holistic development program that included income generation activity, women's business workshops, youth leadership, health assistant primary health trainings, school and community outreach health programs, clinic services, and sports activities. The income generating aspect of the program required attention to detail and working through many logistical hurdles that are a fact of life when dealing with services for remote islands. But over a three-to-four year period, the NGO-outer island collaboration demonstrated a number of successes. One of these was articulated by Ideto Jonathan, a health worker on one of the islands that partnered with

Youth to Youth in Health. "Young people didn't leave Ulien (Arno Atoll) because they were so busy working," he said. "The girls were making handicrafts, the women were gardening. Youth to Youth in Health started a garden. Everyone was too busy. They didn't want to go anywhere. They were happy where they were." Speaking in an interview with me in 2012 for my recent book, Don't Ever Whisper, Jonathan added, "now, everyone is migrating. Ulien young people are waiting for the next flight to the United States."

Marshall Islands government officials will soon focus significant attention on the third international conference of Small Island States scheduled for Samoa in late 2014 that is expected to craft the Pacific's agenda for the global post-2015 sustainable development agenda. "For the Marshall Islands, the time is ripe for a renewed political commitment to sustainable development," said a National Report issued by the Ministry of Foreign Affairs last May in preparation for the 2014 Sustainable Development summit in Apia. "Looking beyond 2015, there needs to be a fundamental shift in development thinking that better links the global agenda with national development aspirations...we need to own our problems, and understand their root causes, in order to develop effective, culturally sensitive solutions to our development challenges."

The question and the challenge for urban-based decision makers in these small island states is what priority do they place on rural communities and do they appreciate that self-reliance starts at the grassroots level — which in the Pacific islands means remote villages and outer islands.

Lots of talk about 'resilience'

Most aid projects are initiated by donors and urban center-based government officials with little participation from outer islanders and local community leaders in addressing sustainability needs of the country.

The term "resilience" is much in vogue in the world of disaster preparedness and climate action. Donor countries and agencies are today heavily focused on "building resilience" of small island countries. A multitude of in-country workshops and training programs, and multi-nation collaborative projects are being funded to help islands improve their capacity to respond to natural disasters and the existential threat from our changing climate and rising ocean levels.

A key challenge for many islands is that most aid projects are initiated by donors and urban center-based government officials with little participation from outer islanders and local community leaders in addressing sustainability needs of the country. An important question to ask: Who is "resilient" in the Pacific? Certainly not people in the urban centers, which would collapse if container ships stopped arriving in ports to disgorge their cans of corned beef, bags of rice, and cases of cola. People living in villages outside urban centers or on remote islands depend to a greater degree today on imported goods than in years past. But if the ships stopped coming, outer islanders would survive while their urban cousins wouldn't.

An even more significant effect on development planning is that within the past 30 years, there has been heavy migration into Pacific island cities, with demographics changing in many islands from majority of people in remote areas to increasing numbers in the centers. The Marshall Islands is a prime example: In the 1960s, 75 percent of the population lived outside of Majuro and Ebeye, the two urban areas. Today, it's exactly the opposite. In contrast to earlier generations of leaders and government officials who led the islands from the 1960s to the 1990s, today in many islands a majority of people are born and raised in the centers totally disconnected from their outer island roots. What this means is the younger generation of government staff managing development projects don't have a connection to the rural areas and this is reflected in urban-centered development planning.

An Asian Development Bank report issued in 1997, "Supporting and Sustaining Fisheries in the Marshall Islands: A Sociological Report," made the observation: "Some government officials are out of touch with community realities, shielded by their high salaries and lives in urban centers, their frequent trips overseas." Written in the late 1990s, but it is certainly descriptive of the state of affairs in many governments today.

In a report I wrote for the Japan International Cooperation Agency (JICA) in 1998, on decentralized and participatory development, I observed: "The vast majority of goals, objectives and action plans for everything from fisheries to family planning are written by outside consultants." This situation is even more pervasive today. And if one thing is true, 99 percent of outside consultants know even less about outer island needs and challenges than the urban islander.

We talk about "resilience" all the time in workshops and funding proposals, but we generally ignore the population that is most resilient: outer islanders and rural villagers. One hundred years ago, when a cyclone swept through, there was no International Red Cross or U.S. Agency for International Development to swoop in with food, water and other aid. Life was harder, but traditional systems were honed over centuries so that islanders could live on the most remote, resource-poor atoll. These traditional systems, many of which are still in practice in rural areas, conserve coastal fisheries, manage agriculture crops, and govern teaching of navigation, canoe building and local medicine. It seems to me, we have a lot to learn about resilience from outer islanders, and should be incorporating traditional systems into resource management because they have worked for centuries. Yet most aid projects deliver things — solar lights, water catchment tanks, small fishing boats — to outer islanders instead of involving them in the development "conversation."

The University of the South Pacific operates a Pacific Centre for Environment and Sustainable Development but sustainable development centers seem to be few and far between in the island region. Institutionalizing community participation in development requires ongoing educational programs about sustainable development and access to information about resources available for community development. Most islands have no center for community-based development activities that could act as a catalyst and entry point for engagement with the wider community. A reoccurring complaint of community representatives, particularly in the outer islands, is that not only don't they have easy access to resources, they don't even know who to ask or where to look for opportunities, skills training, and technical assistance. And it's obvious why: those are concentrated in urban centers by urban-centered government officials.

It would make a lot of sense for universities and community colleges in each island to offer sustainable development courses for students and to take the further step to establish centers for sustainable community-based development, which could be integrated with ongoing research and educational programs of these colleges. We need to get out of our urban thinking box, engage rural communities, and talk to the people who are the most resilient in our islands about building resilience elsewhere.

Plenty of opportunities for talk, but can we get some action, too?

When government leaders are expressing concern about the number of regional meetings, you know it's a problem.

The Pacific Islands Forum meeting in Palau at the end of July 2014 issued its standard communiqué, but one that included two important conclusions of the leaders — perhaps seemingly unrelated to the casual reader — that go to the heart of an increasing problem affecting government service delivery in the Pacific: many government workers are spending so much time in meetings, and traveling to and from them, that they have little time leftover to do the work of delivering services in their countries. The upward spiral of regional meetings is, frankly, astounding and one that is increasingly dominating the work schedule of people working throughout government.

Many government workers are off-island a third to half of the year for regional or international meetings. One might reasonably wonder how government employees mandated to implement, for example, health improvement or energy-related projects have time to do their work when they are traveling so often. A diplomat based in Fiji told me recently that the Forum Secretariat sponsors 60 meetings a year. Then there is the Secretariat of the Pacific Community, Secretariat of the Pacific Regional Environment Program, Forum Fisheries Agency, South Pacific Tourism Association and other so-called CROP agencies all have their list of meetings that require the attention of government officials. And this makes no mention of donor countries and institutions such as the Asian Development Bank, World Bank and International Monetary Fund, all of which host a variety of meetings requiring attendance of officials and leaders — or, and nearly as disruptive to the steady flow of routine government operations as off-shore trips by government employees, they send teams of officials on one-to-two-week visits to each island to document the fiscal status and "good governance" policies of the country in question.

The concern about regional meetings, clearly, has risen to the attention of heads of state in the region because it made it into print in the communiqué from the meeting in Palau that ended earlier this month. The communiqué contains the directive "to rationalise ministerial meetings and endorsed the proposed changes to improve cost allocation, focus and time efficiency, and transparency and accountability of meetings...(and) requested all CROP organisations to consult with their governing bodies and non-member partners on participating in a comprehensive review of regional meetings."

Frequent travel is disrupting delivery of services to the public. If anything, it has gotten worse in recent years. Of course, travel isn't the only disruptor of government services: corruption or lack of leadership, for example, undermine government services just as effectively as absent staff.

Nowadays, it seems, meetings are all about preparing for other meetings. The recent Oceania 21 leaders meeting in New Caledonia, for example, was seen by some leaders as a way to build momentum for the global Small Island Developing States (SIDS) summit in Samoa next month, which in turn is a stepping stone to UN Secretary General Ban Ki-moon's one-day climate summit in mid-September before the opening of the General Assembly, which is being touted by island leaders as a key precursor to the global climate summit in 2015.

Further along in the Forum's Palau communiqué is a paragraph that is seemingly unrelated to the meeting issue — but actually is.

An excerpt from the relevant paragraph reads: "Leaders expressed their serious concern for the extremely large number of Sustainable Development Goals (SDGs) and targets being discussed at the global level and called on the global community to strive for a more manageable, achievable and limited number of SDGs with clear and relevant targets." It went on encourage recognition of the "special case" of SIDS and said issues "that have constrained the ability to achieve Millennium Development Goals (MDGs) in some countries" need to be taken into consideration. This is not a small point, considering that 2015 is the target year for implementation of the MDGs, and only five of 14 countries in the Pacific are on track to implement a majority of the MDGs. Three, in fact, are off-track on all seven MDGs.

As the world moves into the "post-MDG" period by adopting a shopping list of the new mantra known as "Sustainable Development Goals," will it end up simply creating a whole new era of meetings to review the implementation of a global 'to-do' punch list that would likely be beyond the capacity of many small islands anyway, but will certainly be if people needed to carry out the work are spending a good bit of time in places like Dubai, Bangkok, Suva, or New York at SDG review meetings?

Some years ago, Pacific island leaders signed onto the Pacific Plan.

It was a catch-all document with nearly 40 priority areas. For the most part, this plan served as a vehicle for regional get-togethers and Forum Secretariat team visits to member countries to check (the usually little) progress in implementing specific Pacific Plan goals. The 'good progress' made toward regional cooperation under the Pacific Plan noted on the Forum Secretariat website could probably be put down almost entirely to meetings at which, no doubt, "regional cooperation" was well displayed. A review of the plan completed earlier this year completely refocused the point of the document from a "plan" to a "framework" on regionalism. Unfortunately, this will probably result in countless new meetings to discuss regionalism when time could be more effectively spent supporting or initiating efforts within individual Forum nations to deliver on MDGs/SDGs such as improved health and education, access to water and sanitation, job creation, and other key quality of life indicators that, for increasingly large numbers of Pacific islanders, have been on a long, steady decline.

Ahmadiyya Muslim community puts down roots in Marshall Islands

'Islam is not coming to this country anymore, it is part of Marshall Islands now.'

On a back road in downtown Majuro, the first Muslim church in the Marshall Islands is a small but growing entity. Although there had been an Ahmadiyya Muslim community in Majuro for a number of years, it wasn't until the religious group decided to cement its relationship with the Marshall Islands by building a mosque that it began drawing attention — and criticism — of mainstream Christian churches and some political leaders.

Still, the group opened this staunchly Christian nation's first mosque in late 2012 and from this base the Ahmadiyya group is reaching out to the community, particularly working with local youth groups and the Ministry of Health through its partner organization, Humanity First.

Majuro Imam Matiullah Joyia has continuously emphasized the group's rejection of "jihad by the sword" to distinguish the organization from Islamic groups involved in terrorism around the world. It's an important point for Marshall Islanders who pride themselves on their long-standing ties and special relationship with the United States, which includes supporting globally unpopular U.S. positions on the Middle East and Israel at the United Nations. The Marshall Islands' close relationship with the United States government also includes hundreds of Marshallese being past and present members of the U.S. Armed Forces, with many having served multiple tours of duty in Iraq and Afghanistan.

The growing presence of the Ahmadiyya, their active use of government radio like other religious groups, and anti-Islam views of Christian churches and leaders has sparked repeated criticism of the group, criticism ranging from a debate over their right to exist in the Marshall Islands — despite a constitution that guarantees religious freedom — to "concern" over beliefs as expressed in the Quran.

In the two years since establishment of the mosque, Ahmadiyya spokesmen have generally responded to the criticisms in a conciliatory, non-confrontational way by simply explaining the Quran and their philosophy. But the gloves came off earlier this year following criticism by a number of members of parliament during live-broadcast sessions. One senator said the "serious problem" of Muslims being in the Marshall Islands needed to be addressed immediately, while another said the Muslims didn't believe in god and might be doing "something bad" in the future.

A representative of the Ahmadiyya Muslim Community USA, in comments published in the Marshall Islands Journal, asked pointedly: "If a Buddhist prays to a different form of God, can he not meditate in the Marshall Islands? If an atheist denounces the mere existence of God, will the bill of rights not work in his favor? Or if a Baha'i claims belief in Bahaullah will he not be a Marshallese? All such beliefs exist in the Marshall Islands. I tell you today that Islam is a religion of Peace, it means peace and all of its teachings bring mankind towards peace."

The Marshallese General Secretary of the Ahmadiyya Muslim Community, Romeo Tenson, was more direct: "I am a Marshallese and I am a proud Muslim of the Ahmadiyya Community. Islam is not coming to this country anymore, it is part of Marshall Islands now and it is in my blood and in the blood of my fellow Muslim brothers and sisters. I want to tell my family and government that Ahmadiyya Muslim changed my life."

Critics, he said, should be thanking them for their community services including paying for many students to go to school, providing daily lunches and dinners for dozens of children and adults, bringing in specialist doctors to work at the hospital, and holding blood drives.

The historical backdrop to the Ahmadiyya's increasingly active presence offers some food for religious thought. Congregational missionaries from the United Church of Christ in the U.S. established the first Christian church in 1857 in the far-flung Marshalls' outpost of Ebon Atoll. The missionaries translated the Bible into Marshallese and trained local church leaders while spreading the gospel to all inhabited islands. Until just before the turn of the century, the UCC was the only church in the islands. Then the Catholics set up a small, but active presence that was interrupted during Japanese rule between World War I and World War II.

The Catholics, under Jesuit leadership, returned after World War II and began a decades-long focus on building schools in several islands and delivering quality education, educational efforts that continue today. The dominant UCC and smaller Catholic Church coexisted as the only churches in the country — until the 1960s, when the evangelical Assembly of God entered the picture. Since then, the Christian church landscape has dramatically changed.

While still the largest church in numbers, the UCC has seen major membership inroads into populations it once led by the Assembly of God and several of its offshoots. A Baha'i group established itself in the 1970s and has continued to grow despite early criticism from mainstream Christians that is similar in nature to that aimed at the Ahmadiyya Muslims today. The Church of Jesus Christ of Latter-Day Saints (Mormons) established its first "stake" in Majuro in 2009 when it met the minimum membership of over 4,000 members, and has stepped up its community service options, continuing to attract new members.

A hallmark of both the LDS church and the Ahmadiyya Muslim community is their focus on programs benefiting the wider community. These have ranged from regular blood donation drives for the hospital and community service work to English language and computer classes and sponsorship of sports competitions. These community-based programs that are not confined to their immediate church members distinguish these two religious groups from many of the dominant Christian religions and are obviously an entry point for recruiting new members. High unemployment and school drop out rates and a general dissatisfaction with the status quo in an economically stagnant country make for fertile recruitment territory for religious — or other — organizations offering opportunities, educational options and related activities.

It may be a while before the Ahmadiyya are accepted or recognized by leaders of Christian churches and some government leaders. But there is no doubt that, like other religious groups before them, the Ahmadiyya has planted roots and is growing in number.

Chapter 3: What happened to 'Good Governance?'

'Good governance' is an elusive goal where institutional capacity and political will for change are limited. Photo: Tobolar Copra Processing Authority.

Human trafficking a growing issue in the Pacific islands

Lack of opportunities for young people and increasing poverty in urban centers makes a fertile environment for sex trade to expand.

Nearly half of the independent Pacific island countries are evaluated by the United States State Department's 2013 Trafficking in Persons list, and four of these seven are either "Tier 2 Watch List" or "Tier 3," the worst ranking.

Pacific islands should care about their ranking in the Trafficking in Persons (TIP) annual listing because it is an evaluation of border control, enforcement of laws, and systems and services to address prostitution, child abuse, and related trafficking issues.

The State Department evaluated 189 nations globally in its 2013 report released recently and only 29 are on the Tier 1, which designates countries that fully comply with the minimum standards of the Trafficking Victims Protection Act, a U.S. law. A majority of countries are on Tier 2, which acknowledges a country is making "significant efforts" to meet minimum trafficking prevention standards, but does not fully comply. Tier 2 Watch List designates that the number of victims is significant or increasing, and there was no evidence shown of increasing efforts to combat severe forms of trafficking since the previous year. The Watch List is a warning that a country could be demoted to Tier 3, where financial sanctions could apply for not meeting minimum prevention standards and not making efforts comply.

Fiji, Palau and Tonga have maintained a Tier 2 ranking over the past three years. Papua New Guinea, the only Tier 3 ranking in the Pacific islands, has not been able to improve its lowest ranking in several years. The Federated States of Micronesia was Tier 3 in 2011, but moved up to Tier 2 Watch List for the past two years. The Solomon Islands has bounced back and forth: Tier 2 Watch List in 2011, improved to Tier 2 in 2012, and was demoted back to Watch List this year. Marshall Islands was also Tier 2 the last two years, but dropped to Watch List status this year. These countries are among the 44 Tier 2 Watch List countries in the 2013 TIP report.

What does it all mean? Each country report identifies different issues the State Department, through its embassies, identifies. This year's report on the Marshall Islands, for example, said: "The Republic of the Marshall Island is a destination country for women from East Asia subjected to sex trafficking...The government made no efforts to prevent trafficking during the year. It did not conduct any public campaigns or take other steps to raise public awareness about the dangers of trafficking."

A baseline issue that improves a country's image is simply modernizing legislation to reflect human trafficking as a problem, with relevant penalties. Palau, for example, has adopted its own trafficking law, and officials in the Marshalls and FSM report they are working on their own legislation. For many of these small islands, the issue simply hasn't been on the radar. Generally people view human trafficking as a problem in Asia or Africa. But, as an article in the August issue of Islands Business pointed out under the headline, "PNG a haven for sex trafficking," there is an emerging problem of teenage — and younger — girls employed in nightclubs as hostesses, dancers and bartenders.

With high unemployment rates in most urban centers in the region, the extended family system increases the burden on the few wage earners, who, in some cases, eject non-productive extended family members from their homes. Even in the smaller islands, as people migrate to the urban centers and family units break up, more young people of both genders are ending up virtually homeless — they may bounce around to the homes of different relatives — and having to fend for themselves. Lack of opportunities for young people and increasing poverty in urban centers makes a fertile environment for sex trade to expand.

A point made as part of the recommendation of the State Department's TIP report on the Marshalls states: "Take steps to prosecute public officials when there is evidence they are complicit in trafficking activities or hindering ongoing trafficking prosecutions." This hints at a broader issue that could be a roadblock to improvement in some countries worldwide that are on Tier 2 Watch List or Tier 3 status: Are local residents in government or business actively engaged in or benefiting from human trafficking and sex trade practices?

The "stick" behind the State Department's TIP ranking is that Tier 3 status can involve cuts to foreign aid to a government. A country has two years to show improvement in Tier 2 Watch List status, but provided it is making progress, it can remain in this status for up to four years. After this, without requisite improvement, it is automatically downgraded to Tier 3.

If any of the three U.S.-affiliated north Pacific nations end up in Tier 3, the funding package under the 20-year Compact of Free Association would not be affected, but other U.S. federal programs

— to which they are eligible — could be cut. For any nation in Tier 3, this could include withholding aid other than for humanitarian or trade purposes, and U.S. government opposition to some aid from international financial institutions such as the International Monetary Fund and the World Bank.

The State Department's punch list for combating human trafficking: Train law enforcement and judicial officials to implement new anti-trafficking laws; increase efforts to investigate, prosecute, and punish trafficking offenders and apply stringent sentences to convicted offenders; work with NGOs and international organizations to provide protective services to victims; make efforts to study human trafficking in the country; adopt proactive procedures to identify victims of trafficking among vulnerable groups, such as foreign workers and women in prostitution; develop and conduct anti-trafficking information and education campaigns; accede to the 2000 United Nations Trafficking in Persons Protocol.

It's a lot of work. But the point is for governments, with the engagement of NGOs, to establish systems for preventing abuses against people, particularly minors, and providing safety nets. And there is precedent for solving this type of international blacklisting.

In the late 1990s, the Financial Action Task Force (FATF) blacklisted several Pacific nations for being "non-cooperative" with anti-money laundering programs. The Cook Islands, Marshall Islands, Nauru, and Niue were among 15 nations blacklisted globally. This blacklisting motivated the Marshall Islands, for example, to establish an interagency group in government that went to work on FATF recommendations and over the next several years implemented many of them — updating legislation, establishing a Financial Intelligence Unit, and engaging with international anti-money laundering groups, such as the Asia Pacific Group. In several years, the Marshalls got off the blacklist and has stayed off.

In light of the many factors in our islands' urban centers that have marginalized a recognizable number of citizens, creating opportunities for sex and human trafficking abuses, the State Department's report should be seen as identifying problems and offering a road map for improving the safety of both local and foreign residents alike.

Travel mentality takes over in the islands

The increasing frequency of travel disrupts delivery of services to the public.

In the development world of Pacific governments, NGOs, and donor agencies, overseas travel is little discussed but frequently undertaken. The list of conferences, workshops, program reviews, and trainings seems to multiply each year such that mid-level managers and politicians are able to spend close to half the year on the road — and frequently do.

The question, simply, is what benefit does the public from all the trips taken by government personnel? The benefits to the islanders who get on the travel circuit are numerous, but does it result in anything happening back home? Indeed, in some countries, such as the Marshall Islands, government workers are allowed to keep the frequent flyer mileage they accumulate, often in the hundreds of thousands of miles per year — which offers additional free travel. As Palau's special prosecutor demonstrated a few years ago, political leaders often piggybacked personal travel on official travel, with government footing the bill for both the additional airfare and per diem.

Often we find out about this travel on Facebook, as people post news of their travel to exotic locations: we see government people in Dubai, Tokyo, New York, Rome, London. Photos of people hoisting cocktails, standing in front of scenic attractions or feet up on the seats in business class seem to be the Facebook norm.

Because there is increased sensitivity among the public about the high cost of international travel, government officials when issuing media releases about the travel often highlight the fact that the trip was paid for by a donor. But this misses an important point: when government workers are away for weeks on end, it means they are not at home to implement programs and deliver services for the public. A not atypical conversation with someone in government these days goes like this:

Caller: Can we get together in the next few days to talk about this upcoming project?

Government official: I'm leaving on a trip in three days can we do it when I get back?

Caller: When do you return?

Government official: In about two weeks.

So the caller waits the two weeks, then adds a couple more days, since quite often government officials do not return to work the day of their arrival or even the next day. Because the government worker has been away, he or she is difficult to reach because postponed meetings have multiplied and numerous people are competing for time. When the caller finally gets through, it turns out the government worker is about to depart on another trip and so another couple of weeks goes by before they can get together. In the government reality of the 21st century, it can take months to meet with a government worker.

Oddly enough, while most people — at least in the under-40 generation — are oriented to Facebook, posting frequent updates as they travel, it is often difficult to get them to respond to emails. On their return home, they reply to inquiries by apologizing for having been away. Yet in the digital world of email, where we are is of little consequence to maintaining communication. Yet travel seems to be an excuse for disengaging on the part of some government officials.

In recent years, fisheries officials have been required to travel almost as much as those in foreign affairs. Fisheries treaty negotiations with the United States and the European Union, technical and annual meetings with the Secretariat of the Pacific Community, Forum Fisheries Agency, Western and Central Pacific Fisheries Commission, and the Parties to the Nauru Agreement (PNA) itself occupy many weeks in every year. But in the eight PNA member nations at least, we have seen the benefit being brought home from these meetings: revenue to PNA members has quadrupled over the past four years as a consequence of PNA fisheries management actions.

But the benefits of government trips related to health and social services are less obvious, particularly as these government departments are on the front line of providing services to the public. When high officials or program staff in these areas is gone for three-to-four months a year, their programs suffer at home. Other staff will often apologize to their customers that they cannot make a decision or take action on a request until their supervisor returns from a trip.

The fact is that at least some of the one-week type trainings offered — "production of information, education and communication (IEC) materials," "using the media effectively," etc. — are of little value to government officials who are more focused on enjoying their trip than working. Photos abound of U-shaped meeting tables with dozens of officials sitting around, many with laptops on the table. How many of those computers are tuned into Facebook (or some other program) unrelated to the content of the meeting? Far too many, is my observation from attending some workshops. So if some at these workshops are engaged in social media while the training is proceeding, it's pretty obvious that they won't be able to bring much home from the workshop.

Finally, audits in the Marshall Islands have from time to time noted that government does not always enforce the requirement that an employee submit an acceptable trip report before being eligible to receive the 15 percent balance due for their trip per diem. And even if an employee did produce a cursory report, did recommendations and information from the overseas travel get disseminated to other staff in their office or to other agencies that might benefit from the information? It appears that in many government offices, this doesn't happen.

The trip becomes the goal instead of being viewed as a stepping-stone to something else (access to grants or technical assistance, for example).

It is obvious that without government leadership that understands it needs its employees at home to deliver services, the overseas trip engine will continue on its present track. Certainly, attendance at some overseas activities is necessary and even important. But rethinking the number of overseas trips and the number of people who travel, sapping the strength of limited personnel in small islands, merits attention of governments in the region.

The aid and sovereignty debate in the FSM and Marshall Islands

While political leaders argue their sovereignty case publicly, bloated bureaucracies, that are good for the employees but not too much else, do not help their case.

A debate over United States donor aid to the Marshall Islands and Federated States of Micronesia is intensifying as island leaders chafe at controls being exerted by the United States government. The President of the FSM and the Foreign Minister of the Marshall Islands frame their criticism as a sovereignty issue: We're independent countries — don't dictate aid terms to us. Yet this position, as attractive as it may seem, overlooks fiscal and political developments in the United States. The U.S. government's Interior Department administers the millions of dollars provided under 20-year funding agreements that are part of Compacts of Free Association with the two north Pacific nations. Interior is under increasing pressure from the U.S. Congress and the Government Accountability Office (GAO) to show that the funding is producing measurable improvements in education and health and being managed accountably.

During the 2013 Pacific Islands Forum in Majuro, FSM President Emmanuel Mori told me the FSM's relationship with the United States "has been very good. But the implementation level is a thorn." For the first time in nearly 30 years of Compact relations, the U.S. and Marshall Islands have been unable to reach agreement on a Compact budget allocation for the new fiscal year (that starts October 1, 2013), which has put the country's entire national budget process in limbo. The U.S. is putting conditions on Compact funding, but the Marshall Islands does not want funds to be subject to any restrictions. "Full Compact grant allocations should be an annual allocation and disbursed with no conditions," Foreign Minister Phillip Muller said in August. The United States, said Mori, "still treats us like one of the territories. My honest view is it is a conflict to follow established rules that don't necessarily respect our sovereignty."

The first Compacts were implemented for the Marshall Islands and FSM in 1986. While they included broad goals for increasing economic self-reliance for these islands of the former United

Nations Trust Territory, the initial Compacts were largely a political arrangement — one that ended territorial status and helped underwrite newly established governments in Pohnpei and Majuro. Politically, they were a success; economically, less so. Throughout the first 15 years of funding, there was little emphasis on "performance" and "accountability" by the U.S. government. As the funding agreement came up for renegotiation in 1999-2000, a GAO team conducted its first serious audit of the $2.6 billion the U.S. provided FSM and the Marshall Islands from 1986-2001. The title of the GAO report, "Better Accountability Needed Over U.S. Assistance to Micronesia and the Marshall Islands," explains the result of the audit. It had the immediate impact of motivating U.S. State Department negotiators to ratchet up accountability and performance requirements in the second Compact funding agreement that went into force in 2003. Among the key elements of the current Compacts' funding arrangements are the Joint Economic Management Committee (JEMCO) for the FSM and the Joint Economic and Financial Accountability Committee (JEMFAC) for Marshall Islands. The U.S. maintains a three-to-two majority on these committees that are mandated to meet annually to review and approve Compact funding allocations.

Many political leaders in both island countries cut their teeth during the free-spending days of the original Compact when government jobs were viewed as a way to share the aid wealth. Today, the Interior Department is increasingly demanding that the governments show they are planning for the future — the funding agreement ends in 2023 — and that Compact funding is producing improvements in health and education, the focus of the funding. The problem from the U.S. government's perspective is that the national governments are not addressing how to deal with their heavy dependence on the annual U.S. Compact grants that decline each year until they end in 2023, and most of their performance indicators are unreliable.

While political leaders argue their sovereignty case publicly, bloated bureaucracies, that are good for the employees but not too much else, do not help their case. An ongoing lack of performance by many government personnel is compounding development challenges at a time of when action is urgently needed. The lack of national leadership on these problems is evident in the chronically poor management at the Ministry of Health in Majuro, which spends over 20 percent of the country's budget each year — much of it from Compact and other U.S. government sources. Do government leaders not care that day-to-day service in many government departments is poor despite huge infusions of donor aid, or is it they don't know how to fix problems and engage government personnel to perform, or at a minimum show up to work 40 hours a week? Either way, the inability of national governments in the Marshall Islands and FSM to greatly improve progress in health and education isn't just a donor issue. It goes to the heart of national development goals and their implementation. Despite donor assistance accounting for more than 60 percent of their annual budgets, and most of it focused in health, education and poverty-reduction areas, these two nations are on track to meet just two of the eight Millennium Development Goals — in contrast to Palau, their neighbor and Compact of Free Association partner with the U.S., which is on track to implement seven of the eight. Both countries' arguments about sovereignty would be bolstered by performance. But to date, in the public sector, it is largely absent. For example, the GAO says only one of 14 education indicators was "capable of demonstrating progress," while in health the majority of indicators were found to be unreliable as a way to measure performance.

The GAO, which reports directly to the U.S. Congress, in its September 20, 2013 report, recommended that the Interior Department take all necessary steps to ensure that the Marshall Islands and FSM complete satisfactory plans to address annual decrements in Compact funds, produce reliable indicator data used to track progress in education and health, and address all single audit findings in a timely manner. At the annual JEMFAC and JEMCO meetings last month with the Marshall Islands and FSM, respectively, the U.S. Interior Department listed these as priority requirements that had to be acted on and supported use of U.S. funding to do so.

While island leadership is increasingly vocal against what it sees as over-reaching U.S. oversight of Compact funding, a better measure of sovereignty would be improved government performance and a pace of implementation in health and education commensurate with the level of donor assistance. This is what local populations urgently need to help develop solutions to such problems as non-communicable diseases that have risen to the point that in 2012 President Loeak declared NCDs to be a national emergency.

Ad hoc decisions don't make it in an increasingly complex world

Ad hoc decision-making based on little more than how leaders feel about situations — or which 'fire' is burning brightest — is a continuing obstacle to good governance.

What is worse? Turning government planning and implementation over to consultants who drop in for a few weeks at a time, putting it in the hands of people without the tools or inclination to do it, or engaging competent locally based people to provide advice and then ignoring it? This crystallizes the development-planning dilemma that has faced the Marshall Islands for nearly the past 20 years.

Since the mid-1990s — a period that roughly tracks the membership of the Marshall Islands in the Asian Development Bank — the Marshall Islands has increasingly relied on outside consultants to do core planning work for the government. Is it a coincidence that this period has coincided with a glaring lack of performance in government, which shows in many areas, including slow progress on meeting Millennium Development Goals?

In the 1980s and into the early 1990s, by contrast, the Marshall Islands hired skilled planners, not only in its national planning office, but within individual ministries. Times have changed dramatically since Dr. H.M. Gunasekera produced the first two five-year development plans for the Marshall Islands beginning in the mid-1980s. While Dr. Gunasekera was from Sri Lanka, he lived permanently in Majuro for many years and was embedded in the government structure as the chief planner. The five-year plans his office produced were a product of daily consultation with and involvement by the government apparatus, and reflected the situation on the ground.

The contrast with the 1990s and 2000s is dramatic. In today's world, consultants drop in for a couple of weeks at a time, generate reports, get paid and little gets done as a result of their strategic planning. One example is the Ministry of Education — an entity with the most personnel with graduate degrees — that in the mid-2000s hired three outside experts to produce its five-year strategic plan. They did. But did anyone read the detailed, matrix-oriented document? In light of poor public school performance in the late 2000s, it is evident the plan had little impact on the school system.

In 2013, the Marshall Islands government hired a U.S.-based consultant to help produce a government-wide strategic plan. In early October, the Pacific Islands Forum Secretariat announced the availability of a consultancy for the Marshall Islands for producing a strategic planning document. Will these consultants competently deliver the required report? No doubt. Will anything much result? If the past is a guide, there is little doubt about the answer: no.

This is not an issue unique to the Marshall Islands. The lack of planning capacity in governments and the heavy reliance on consultants to produce core government documents and plans is also prevalent in the Federated States of Micronesia and other islands in the region.

The Marshall Islands government does so little of its own planning that it created, in the mid-2000s, two commissions to review government spending and its tax regime. These two groups included significant local participation. The Comprehensive Adjustment Program issued a report in 2009 that listed numerous opportunities for the government to reduce spending and the size of its workforce in a systematic way that would contribute to the sustainability of government operations. Virtually nothing was implemented from these recommendations. Meanwhile, a tax reform plan was proposed around the same time and is moving forward with substantial Australian aid, in large part because it fits free-trade plans for the region with its substitution of a value added tax in place of import duties. Perhaps the message here is simple: a) governments won't cut spending or address sustainability unless crises force their hand and b) if you can get donor funding, you can get traction on a plan — at least while donor interest lasts.

But the larger point is that old style, ad hoc decision-making based on little more than how leaders feel about situations — or which "fire" is burning brightest — is a continuing obstacle to good governance based on planning, research and effective locally-based involvement and implementation. Then, too, many government officials in the U.S.-affiliated Pacific see performance reports and planning documents as a grant game — a requirement to be met as quickly as possible and, once submitted, filed in cabinet.

In 2005, the first-ever performance audit conducted in the Marshalls was a review of public education with funding from ADB. It was an unusual effort by a consultant working with a locally-based counterpart. Under the title, "Increasing ownership and effective demand for improved education," the study broke new ground by identifying in detail the many foundational impediments to improving public education in the country. Since public schools have been a black hole eating resources but generating little in academic output for 30 years, it was refreshing to see a report that offered a roadmap of areas in need of action. Despite the quality of this report, however, it followed the path of virtually every other consultant's report: it was of little interest to either the Marshall Islands Ministry of Education or the U.S. Interior Department, which funds most of the ministry's budget, and now sits as a historical document — the first performance audit conducted in the Marshall Islands — on the ADB website.

Part of the issue is insistence on hiring Marshall Islanders for key positions even if no one is trained or qualified for a particular position in government. It's understandable in the post-colonial period in the region, but doesn't lead to improved governance. No doubt, a list could be produced in every island of positions that would benefit from appointment of qualified outsiders — the smaller the island, the longer the list. In the Marshalls, these include the Attorney General and Majuro Hospital management. In most small islands, there are skill gaps: people have never been trained in certain areas (hospital management) or island culture undermines the ability of a local person to implement the duties of a post (Attorney General) that requires frequent use of the word "no."

The notable education problems in the Marshall Islands coupled with visa-free status that allow people to live, study and work in the United States, have produced an extremely high dropout rate from college. There are not enough Marshall Islanders trained to fill all the urgently needed skilled positions.

It's pretty clear that the Marshall Islands and other island governments that rely heavily on consultants need to rethink this strategy, begin hiring fulltime skilled people into key planning and oversight posts in government, and focus on getting islanders trained in these essential posts. This is essential if we want strategic planning that matches conditions on the ground and has local ownership for action that translates into results.

Reform agenda grows long in north Pacific

Each year of delayed reform raises the specter of more difficult choices to come.

Signs of the times: In he late 1980s, a nighttime drive around Majuro in December revealed the shining splendor of Christmas: house after house was covered in glittering, blinking lights. The Christmas Day celebration too was one of enjoyable and extravagant celebration: dozens of groups performing dances and songs in churches throughout the country. The performances invariably concluded with the dancers tossing literally hundreds of pounds of candy, sweets and other gifts to a wildly scrambling audience.

How times have changed. Christmas 2013 offered a clear barometer of economic conditions — better than any written report could. Perhaps one in 50 Majuro homes strung Christmas lights outside and most of the businesses that did have holiday light displays put up the obligatory minimum to mark the season. And candy tossing during the Christmas celebration was the exception, not the rule, at this year's Christmas. As the cost of mounting a Christmas group, known as "jepta" in the Marshall Islands, has escalated, fewer non-church community-based groups perform in recent years. The costs of uniforms, feeding jepta members who practice on a nightly basis for six-to-eight-weeks, the cost of transport to move everyone to and from practice and performances, and finally, the donation of food and other gifts to the different churches where jeptas perform has put the job of mounting a jepta out of financial reach of people who a generation ago eagerly joined in by organizing a group for the Christmas celebration in the Marshall Islands. The 2013 Christmas celebration did not lack for spirit. But for anyone watching and participating in jeptas since the 1980s, the change is obvious, and clearly driven by economics.

The government, in contrast, deployed a new and elaborate light display at its capital building to mark the 2013 holiday season. Superficially, at least, it suggests an underlying disconnect on the part of political leaders with the significant change that has altered life for the worse for many in the population. It may also be a metaphor for the lack of initiative on clearly needed reforms in government operations by successive governments in the Marshall Islands. It is possible that people in government with access to numerous financial resources have yet to come to terms with the poverty and hardship affecting various sectors of society.

This situation is understandable in light of how government bureaucracies grew in the Marshall Islands as well as the Federated States of Micronesia and Palau. Government employment was a way to distribute aid and developed during a time of considerable U.S. economic largesse in the 1980s and 1990s. Government workers generally didn't have to meet performance goals or even show up to work regularly to get their paychecks. Times have changed. Today, donors have ratcheted up aid requirements as they demand performance results for money provided, while cutting back on grants for personnel.

Looking ahead to 2014 and beyond — and particularly for the Marshalls and FSM, whose 20-year financial packages in their Compacts of Free Association with the U.S. expire in 2023 — the question of increasing significance is will the governments engage in meaningful reform to improve government work performance, economic conditions, and health, education and social indicators?

Palau has been a leader in the region in political reform measures. More than a decade ago, it created a Special Prosecutor office as a watchdog on government spending. While it had its limitations and in recent years was largely dysfunctional, in its early days the special prosecutor took the first enforcement actions against elected leaders, forcing reimbursements of hundreds of thousands of dollars in public money misused for travel by government leaders. More recently, Palau enacted term limits for the National Congress, a move that has forced long-term members to retire. Whether this has improved legislative governance may be open to debate, but it does mandate regular turnover of membership.

During 2012 and 2013, the FSM launched a series of state-level consultations to get participation in developing plans for reducing government spending as part of a Long-Term Fiscal Framework to address the decline in U.S. grant funding. "The process," reported the Graduate School USA in its recently released FY2012 FSM Economic Review, "did provide a participatory approach to prioritize expenditures in a comprehensive way." President Emanuel Mori has also established a 2023 Committee to focus on actions needed by government to improve its financial situation in the lead up to the end of U.S. grants, that now underwrite over half of the government's budget.

In the Marshall Islands, reform has been harder to come by. A Comprehensive Adjustment Program (CAP) task force appointed by the President issued a report to Cabinet in 2009 outlining numerous measures that could be taken to reduce government spending and improve the national government budget process. The FY2012 Economic Review of the Marshall Islands, issued late in 2013 by the Graduate School USA, noted that: "None of the last four budgets has been consistent with the CAP recommendations." Plans for major tax reform, overhaul of state owned enterprise operations, changes to the retirement law to stave off bankruptcy of the social security system, and other public sector reforms have been in the planning stages for several years without moving to implementation.

While Jaluit representative Alvin Jacklick was Speaker of parliament from 2009-2011, he formulated a Nitijela Corporate Plan that called for numerous government reforms, including reducing the 33-member parliament to 20 members. The report was largely ignored. The Marshalls has gained help from the Asian Development Bank, Pacific Islands Forum Secretariat and other donors to engage consultants to write various national development strategies, but the lack of ownership of these plans leads to the obvious question: If government has not implemented recommendations of the CAP task force, which was a largely homegrown effort, what level of implementation will result from strategies produced by expatriates?

The parliament came under increasing public pressure in 2014 to sponsor the first constitutional convention in nearly 20 years. Speaker Donald Capelle established a special committee to review the need for a constitutional convention, and the committee's report could not be clearer: the public is clamoring for constitutional reform, everything from rewriting the parliamentary style of government in favor of direct election of the president and a halt on selling land, to establishment of a special prosecutor and ombudsman to combat corruption. Despite calls for a con-con in recent years, successive governments have avoided doing so. This will be a major issue for the Marshall Islands parliament in 2014 — whether or not to accede to the expressed wishes of the public for a con-con. If the parliament adopts legislation to sponsor a constitutional convention, it will mark the first major national consultation in over a decade. If it doesn't happen in 2014, it appears unlikely it will happen in 2015, an election year.*

Whether governments in Majuro, Pohnpei and Koror implement significant reforms, the problems will only worsen each year in the absence of government policy action. Each year of delay raises the specter of more difficult choices to come.

Palau's booming tourist industry, with over 100,000 arrivals annually the past several years, coupled with its regional environmental leadership has opened the door to economic opportunities that have eluded the FSM and Marshall Islands, and gives Palau some options unavailable to its Micronesian neighbors. In addition, despite U.S. assistance accounting for more than 60 percent of their annual budgets, and most of it focused in health and education, the FSM and Marshall Islands are on track to meet just two of the eight Millennium Development Goals — in contrast to Palau, which is on track to implement seven of the eight.

Although health and education have been the focus of U.S. grant funding the past 10 years, neither the FSM nor Marshall Islands have made significant strides in producing results, with communicable diseases such as tuberculosis and Hansen's Disease major problems, and an epidemic of non-communicable diseases battering island populations and government finances. This impacts both nations, and also plays out in relations with the U.S. with about 30 percent of Marshall Islanders and Micronesians now living in the U.S. Some American states as well as Guam and the federal government are raising concern over costs to provide health care, education and social services and this, in turn, is causing some friction in relations between Washington and Pohnpei and Majuro.

Another key question for the Marshall Islands and FSM is whether trust funds established by their Compacts will be able to match U.S. grants that end in 2023. Both trust funds are below benchmarks. The current sufficiency estimate for the FSM trust fund at the end of FY2023 is $1.68 billion. But based on its current value, the FSM trust fund is expected to be nearly half a billion dollars short of this mark in 2023. The Marshall Islands trust fund is closer to being on the mark. The sufficiency estimate for the Marshall Islands trust fund is $745 million, but is projected to fall short by about $40 million in 2023.

Chuuk state in the FSM faces numerous fiscal problems undermining public services, with budget deficits the norm for many years. In the past year, Chuuk established an Advisory Group on Education Reform to navigate a system that has stymied public school improvements. It includes U.S. and island government officials, as well as educators from Palau and elsewhere, bringing high-profile attention to the education sector. Since its formation, the group has broken ground by reviving an education reform agenda. "We feel we have moved significantly forward in our efforts to overcome a variety of obstacles to building and improving schools here in Chuuk," said U.S. Interior Department official Tom Bussanich, a member of the group. "It is our hope that these efforts will result in the construction of numerous schools (in 2014) to the benefit of students, teachers and the broader community."

Palau President Tommy Remengesau, Jr. wants Palau's 200-mile exclusive economic zone turned into a "total marine sanctuary" by halting commercial tuna fishing. Meanwhile, one bright light is fisheries. The membership of these three north Pacific nations in the Parties to the Nauru Agreement (PNA) has seen fisheries revenue skyrocket in four years, a boon to the island nations and their stressed national budgets.

The challenge facing political leaders in these north Pacific countries, leaders who for the most part are on four-year election cycles so generally have a short-term outlook, is starting or continuing to implement minimum reforms and building momentum for 'good governance' that can help improve delivery of health and social services, while increasing the quality of life for citizens in these nations.

* Legislation to authorize holding a constitutional convention was introduced into the Nitijela in September 2014, but had not received a public hearing or been reported out of committee through mid-2015 despite being introduced by a majority of Nitijela members. Legislation introduced before and after this bill was the subject of public hearings and, in a number of cases, adoption.

State Owned Enterprises can be reformed

How is it that in a poorly performing SOE environment, the Marshall Islands government's national utility company has gone from losing approximately $20 million from FY2004-FY2012 to an operating profit of US$2.1 million in FY2013?

With political will, good management, and the right board structure, state owned enterprises (SOEs) can function accountably and effectively. But it is not happening in many islands in the Pacific today. Yet in most parts of the region, SOEs — everything from government-run airlines to ports authorities to utility companies — exercise key functions of government. Lack of transparency and under-performance is the norm, though there are notable exceptions.

A study of SOEs by the Asian Development Bank pointed out that from FY2002-FY2010, SOEs in Fiji, Marshall Islands and Solomon Islands had a negative return on equity, while Samoa's was barely positive at 0.3 percent. While Papua New Guinea's rate of return on equity was 4.2 percent and Tonga's 5.6 percent, ADB commented: "In each country, this rate is substantially below the profitability target set by the government and/or a commercially established risk adjusted return. In the Marshall Islands and Solomon Islands, the chronic operating losses of the SOEs require regular capital infusions from the central budget, further weakening their government's fiscal position. In PNG as in the other countries, the poor performance of the SOEs is due to weak governance arrangements, conflicting mandates, the absence of hard budget constraints, and lack of accountability."

Often, political leaders acknowledge the need for reform, encourage studies and preparation of reform plans, but then do not implement them. A key ingredient to success, according to a number of SOE reviews, is removing political involvement in boards and decision-making. When governments allow bad performance by SOEs, they undermine services to the public and increase costs to taxpayers.

In the Marshall Islands in FY2012, for example, all major SOEs suffered net operating losses, with total losses in the sector reaching $14.7 million — a figure over 10 percent of the national government's budget. Air Marshall Islands is a classic example of an under-performing SOE. It has lost money continuously since it was established in 1980. There have been occasional, but usually quickly aborted attempts at reform, some in response to pressure from the private sector — which would benefit from a properly functioning domestic airline. The national government, during the terms of multiple presidents, has repeatedly injected millions of dollars to keep the national airline afloat without requiring changes in operation.

"Public enterprises that run persistent financial losses are often bailed out or supported by national budgets or donors, and often these bail outs occur without any binding requirements for reform or restructuring," said a 2010 review of Marshall Islands SOEs. "This essentially rewards poor performance and virtually ensures that public resources will flow disproportionately to poorly performing entities."

So how is it that in this poorly performing SOE environment, the government's national utility company has gone from losing approximately US$20 million from FY2004-FY2012 to an operating profit of US$2.1 million in FY2013? The most important elements in the case of the Marshalls Energy Company (MEC) — which oversees supply of electricity to the two urban centers and two outer atolls, Wotje and Jaluit, as well as installation of renewable energy around the country — are adherence to a recovery plan and capable management. Although there is political control of the board of directors — a Cabinet minister chairs the board and there are other government officials on the board — the Marshalls Energy Company has a heavy compliment of experienced private sector people on its board.

The company has teetered on the edge of bankruptcy since the late 2000s. It had problems with just about everything: old engines needing urgent overhauls, an estimated 25 percent electricity loss in its distribution system, large uncollectable debt, a tank farm that an IMF report in 2011 warned was so dilapidated that tanks could begin collapsing. MEC management crafted a recovery plan in 2010 and have proceeded to address each problem area in turn, getting low-interest loans to replace high-interest payments, gaining loan payment deferments to allow focus of cash in areas of need, gaining grants to fix engines, buy and install thousands of prepaid power meters, and to start work on distribution losses. Engine rehabilitation cut use of fuel in the power plant, saving hundreds of thousands of dollars each year.

In 2012, MEC had US$2.2 million in uncollectable debt. Last year, use of prepaid meters and aggressive collection turned this into a US$1.5 million positive revenue stream. Overall, by turning an operating profit and gaining millions of dollars in grants, the government utility cut its net deficiency from US$11 million to US$4 million.

The implementation of a recovery plan by the Marshalls Energy Company shows that a troubled SOE can turn itself around. But it has to have a credible plan of action and the will to implement it. The will to change directions in government or SOE operations is frequently short-lived in island governments.

The ADB's 2012 report on SOE reform commented: "In Pacific island countries, political opposition to SOE reform stems from concerns about: (i) the potential loss of patronage; (ii) the loss of direct control over SOEs, which are perceived to be important policy implementation tools; and (iii) potential job losses as SOEs are restructured and made more efficient."

It seems that unless SOEs hit bottom so there is no alternative but to reform or have exceptionally capable management — or a combination of both — there is little progress. Sadly, the Marshalls' utility company's turnaround is the exception, not the rule. But it does show what a state owned agency can do to improve performance, offering a roadmap for other SOEs and government policymakers.

What is so hard about good governance in the Pacific?

The public suffers, whether it's a local government or a traditional leader signing fishing rights away for a few dollars, or national government officials and elected leaders' side-stepping laws, regulations and policies for large-scale loans, projects or appointments.

Why does it seem so difficult in many Pacific island governments to gain political, policy and implementation level action for good governance and the use of what some people like to term "best practice"? Throughout the region, many workers in the civil service and elected leaders seem to view the government as their own private business. There are, of course, exceptions, but they tend to be a minority. The results of this prevalent attitude are apparent in low government work performance and show in health, education and poverty indicators.

A recent commentator said that on average 30 percent of donor aid is wasted through a combination of poor management and theft. My question: Is that all? And if we accept the 30 percent waste figure, what is the collateral waste and damage from the many people engaged in either mismanaging or stealing the aid funding? While busy manipulating funds for personal benefit, those officials are not doing their real jobs, so there is further loss and inefficiency built into the corruption picture. Then, too, poor management and corruption often is not penalized. So it produces a malaise among others — those trying to actually do their jobs in a poor-governance environment — depressing morale and killing incentive to improve performance.

A recent $1.2 billion loan by the Papua New Guinea government, the appointment and then appointment rescinding of an individual with links to Hezbolla by the Marshall Islands as its envoy to UNESCO, Kiribati selling fishing days beyond its allotted share within the eight-member fishing cartel known as PNA, the Nauru government getting rid of judges in its judiciary, the use of civil service apparatus in many islands to hire close relatives of high-ranking government leaders, bribery of government officials to get contracts, approving agreements with foreign companies for extraction of natural resources by signing contracts provided by the companies. What do these disparate actions have in common? Each of these activities, no matter how they are defended, is an example of bad governance. In one way or another, each of these ignores best practice rules, the purpose of which are to benefit the public and reduce abuse of power by those who hold it in the executive and legislative branches.

As recently as 20 years ago, prior to widespread use of Internet and television in the islands, elected leaders and high-level civil servants could make government decisions for personal benefit and it could be months or even years before the public became aware of it.

The Internet age has helped expose corruption by making information more easily accessible. But it doesn't seem to have reduced corruption for fear of exposure and penalty. Is this because often a person being exposed for a corrupt practice does not suffer a penalty (such as going to jail or losing the next election)? Some of this, what I call a "disconnect," is based on what appears to be a belief in some islands that government is, in fact, for the benefit of people who are in it. Obviously, this is an attitude that needs to change if government performance is to change and improve.

Particularly in small islands, where people tend to know everything about everyone, most are reluctant to point the finger at those involved in corrupt practices or even just plain bad management. Why? Partly because a priority of life in small islands is getting along with everyone since you live and work so close together. Another is that there are many shades of corrupt practices or bad management woven into island societies as a result of foreign aid and the adoption of western styles of governance such that some may be reluctant to call others out for fear of having the finger pointed back at them.

Interestingly, this picture might be changing for the better — if "better" means pointing out corruption. With the filing March 20, 2014 of 52 criminal charges against a Majuro pharmaceutical company* related to bribery to gain hospital contracts, a center of corruption is being targeted by the Marshall Islands Attorney General and Auditor General. Many more charges against government workers allegedly involved are expected to follow. Perhaps the key point in the bribery scandal enveloping Majuro hospital is how services and morale have plummeted in recent years as corruption, poor management, broken diagnostic equipment, and lack of supplies and medicines have been the norm, undermining best efforts of doctors and nurses to maintain adequate services and weakening public confidence in the facility. These are the direct manifestations of corruption.

In response to the combination of the Marshall Islands Auditor General's motivation to investigate fraud and the Attorney General's willingness to file criminal charges, people are calling into the AG's and Auditor General's offices with numerous corruption complaints. Will prosecution — even successful prosecution — of a few people cause change and improve honesty and performance of government managers? It did not three years ago, when half a dozen government workers were convicted of stealing hundreds of thousands of dollars in U.S. government grants to the Ministry of Health. The manipulation of Health funds in the Marshall Islands continued.

Bottom line, the public suffers, whether it's a local government or a traditional leader signing fishing rights away for a few dollars, or national government officials and elected leaders' side-stepping laws, regulations and policies for large-scale loans, projects or appointments. Indeed, an example of this is the Marshall Islands government's decision to set up a bank account for its hosting of the 2013 Pacific Islands Forum summit outside of the Ministry of Finance's procurement system, as is constitutionally required. In an early 2015 audit, the country's auditor general reported that spending of nearly all of the over $2 million in the account violated the procurement law of the Marshall Islands. A frontpage headline in the Marshall Islands Journal reporting the results of the audit was headlined: "Donor funds abused."

There is no easy answer to eliminating the most overt corruption, poor management or violations of rule of law.** Having well-staffed auditor, ombudsman and special prosecutor offices can increase oversight of government money and catch some of the corruption. But until people in island communities begin viewing anti-corruption and good governance as a priority, many islands will likely continue muddling along the paths they are on: showing low performance and poor education, health and development indictors despite reasonably high levels of locally-generated resources or donor aid.

* In late December, 2014 Genesis Island Enterprises paid a record fine of $400,000 and was banned from doing business with the Marshall Islands government for 10 years in a court-approved plea bargain.

** The August 29, 2014 edition of the Marshall Islands Journal reported, under the page-one headline, "Ministry of Wealth": "Illegal spending of hundreds of thousands of dollars by the Ministry of Health is reported in the Marshall Islands Auditor General's latest report delivered to Nitijela (parliament) last week. The audit also shows that disarray at the Ministry of Health last year resulted in the ministry reimbursing a donor for funding that the ministry had actually spent...The audit states that violations of the RMI procurement law by the Ministry of Health have been pointed out by auditors every year since 2005."

Government policies, agencies undermine business development

An ADB review of state owned enterprises in PNG concluded that they were crowding out the private sector.

Pacific governments are littered with failed business ventures. But despite the history of failure, governments keep operating business activities in the guise of state owned enterprises or other government agencies.

Elected leaders have a tendency to verbally promote private sector development, then do little to actually implement their words. In fact, many people in business say the most effective way for governments to support the private sector is simple: pay their bills on time. The months — sometimes years — that businesses are forced to wait on payment for legitimately provided services or goods hurts their operations despite governments' professed support for business.

The World Bank's annual "Doing Business" report for 2014 ranks Pacific nations from number 57 (Tonga) to 156 (Federated States of Micronesia) out of 189 countries evaluated for the ease of business operations. The majority of island nations are in the lower half of countries designated as more difficult for businesses activitie — Solomon Islands (97), Palau (100), Papua New Guinea (113), Marshall Islands (114), and Kiribati (122). Tonga and Fiji (62) are the only two in the upper 50 percent of this World Bank review.

Some political leaders like to be the "private sector." It's not unusual in island nations to see some elected leaders with construction companies or other businesses that enjoy government contracts. Observations of this activity from the Marshall Islands show that these business ventures rarely last. We've seen government leaders' construction firms, entertainment businesses, and housing rental operations all die quiet deaths, usually after the person gets out of office and has less opportunity to gain government contracts or is unable to continue repaying government development bank loans.

While smuggling of goods and tax cheating obviously gives those not paying taxes an unfair advantage, government officials engaging in business similarly creates an uneven playing field for businesses that cannot exercise the same clout to advance their business interests.

Then there are the state owned enterprises (SOEs). A 2012 review by the Asian Development Bank of SOEs in PNG concluded that they were "crowding out the private sector" and acted "as a drag on economic growth." The report noted: "In PNG as in the other countries, the poor performance of the SOEs is due to weak governance arrangements, conflicting mandates, the absence of hard budget constraints, and lack of accountability."

The government-owned Air Marshall Islands is a classic example of a dysfunctional SOE. An ADB report in 2003 said: "The financial position of Air Marshall Islands is precarious — it has never made an operating profit and depends heavily on government subsidies." Ten years later, a report said there had been little change: "Air Marshall Islands has been a company in crisis for many years — continually operating at a loss, with government support only on a crisis-management basis, with weak management and government involvement in operations." Despite pleas from the Marshall Islands Chamber of Commerce and donor agencies, the government has shown little interest in either reforming the airline or letting private companies operate domestic air services. This has undermined private sector tourism development because no one can count on planes arriving or departing on schedule. The country's flagship scuba diving destination at Bikini Atoll, for example, shut down in 2008 after a dozen years of increasingly profitable operations after many international divers were repeatedly stranded by irregular air service.

The situation for businesses is so tenuous in some places, companies are reluctant to consider construction contracts that in other locations would have multiple competitors. When Chuuk state in the Federated States of Micronesia in 2009 tendered a US$25 million road and sewer project to be funded by U.S. Compact infrastructure grants, only one company submitted a tender: Pacific International Inc. (PII), a Majuro and Guam-based construction firm used to the vagaries of operating in isolated islands. But even PII with its experience has run afoul of the FSM government agencies overseeing the construction program. After more than four years of work had the project 90 percent complete, the FSM terminated PII in November with over $3 million unpaid for work already performed. An independent engineering report issued recently said design flaws caused the project to be delayed 837 days at an additional cost of US$7.2 million, of which the FSM's Project Management Unit (PMU) approved less than half. The additional time and cost "has come about as a result of mismanagement of the project by the PMU," said the report. It could not have been clearer:

"The owner (FSM government) was found to be in default of the contract for non-payment of amounts contractually and legally due the contractor (PII) and for other reasons," concluded the report by J.M. Robertson, Inc., a Guam-based engineering firm. But the FSM government has lined up another contractor to finish the project and is lobbying the U.S. government to lift a ban on construction funding that was put in place because of concerns about project management. In the meantime, PII will likely take the FSM to court — but will it be able to collect the millions owed for legitimately performed work?* Is it any wonder PII was the only private company to bid on the project in 2009?

The latest government business venture in the Marshall Islands is the soon-to-be-established Office of Commerce and Investment under the Ministry of Resources and Development. The government is apparently investing about half a million dollars from its increasing pot of fishing revenue to launch the new government agency whose mandate is to reinvigorate an economy long sunk in a swamp of malaise. In the late 1980s and 1990s, the government established the Marshall Islands Development Authority whose mandate was business development. It spent a lot of money with little long-term business result. Once again, with its new Office of Commerce and Investment, the government is repeating past practice and hoping for a different result.

Given that government funded initiatives have largely failed, and such efforts as micro-loans, while helpful in a modest way, are unlikely to generate large-scale employment opportunities, what might actually work?

One idea that's largely been ignored in the islands is one promoted for many years by north Pacific business advisor C. L. Cheshire, who is based in Hawaii. Cheshire has been involved in working with and advising numerous government agencies and businesses in the region. His conclusion: the best way to spur economic expansion and job creation in the private sector is to invest in already established businesses that have the human resource and physical infrastructure, and demonstrate business experience and staying power. The idea: inject funding and expertise into existing operations to get them to develop new areas of enterprise — fisheries or agriculture or food processing, for example — or expand on successful ones, such as tourism operations.

A business plan will have a better chance of success if a successful business implements it instead of someone with no business experience, although people with 'start up' plans generally get funding support and interest. Unfortunately, this line of thinking usually runs into a common challenge in small islands: jealousy of success.

One thing is for certain: governments need a new way of thinking about the private sector, one that appreciates the difficulties of doing business in the islands.

* In December 2014, Pacific International Inc. filed suit against the FSM government seeking to recover over $14 million in losses on the Chuuk road project. In March 2015, the lawsuit was put on hold by agreement of both sides to allow for mediation in June 2015. The result of the mediation was favorable to PII, but details of the decision were not available when this book was published.

Donors want performance — or do they?

With corruption undermining development goals and preventing benefits of aid from reaching the community, donors should consider providing resources to government audit and ombudsman offices in the region.

Australian Foreign Minister Julie Bishop laid down the new law on her government's aid program in a major policy shift in June 2014. "The government will introduce a rigorous system of performance benchmarks and mutual obligations tailored to each country's circumstances," said Bishop in her mid-June policy announcement. "When projects don't deliver the results we expect, they will be put on a rigorous path to improvement or be terminated." She repeatedly emphasized "performance" as the guiding goal of Australia's new foreign aid policy, and emphasized support for private sector initiatives to address poverty problems.

Three months before Bishop's announcement, the U.S. government announced its new Pacific American Climate Fund, a US$24 million fund to support climate initiatives over five years. Like the new Australian aid model Bishop announced, the U.S. climate fund is similarly focused on innovation and performance. Unlike the Australians, however, the U.S. climate fund simply removed government involvement entirely: grants are available only to the private sector and non-government organizations.

Even the Republic of China (Taiwan) government is ratcheting up basic aid requirements. Long accused of checkbook diplomacy, Taiwan today — at least with some of its six Pacific diplomatic partners — is requiring detailed reports before it will release next quarter funding. This change in the Marshall Islands has led to major delays in government receiving the quarterly drawdowns of aid in late 2013 and 2014 because of difficulties the government has had in producing the required reports.

The U.S. government's climate fund initiative appears to have taken some lessons from U.S. Compact of Free Association relationships with the Marshall Islands and Federated States of Micronesia where, despite the injection of large sums of funding principally to health and education, improvements in these areas has been slow and in some cases non-existent. Indeed, this is understandable in the Marshalls, which is now seeing its second round of major criminal prosecutions for theft of funds at the

Ministry of Health, the first being in the 2011-12 period. People involved in manipulating the government system for private gain are not focused on achieving "performance benchmarks." In the meantime, the U.S. government continues to press both FSM and Marshall Islands to improve development planning to address the annual decline in U.S. grants leading to the 2023 end of financial assistance under the Compact. This has led to accusations by leaders in both countries of colonial style interference, and ongoing disputes at high levels of government over management of the U.S. aid program. Still, the FSM last year embarked on a state and national budget consultation process for the first time, while leadership in the Marshalls has been largely uninterested in the planning process, simply hiring consultants to produce reports.

Then there is the World Bank, which has been dangling multi-million dollar grants without any conditions attached to get countries such as the Federated States of Micronesia and the Marshall Islands to pass legislation to open their telecommunications sectors to competition. The FSM government was offered $43 million, while the Marshall Islands was offered $13 million to pass legislation to this effect. The money is not tied to the telecom sector and can be spent in any manner by the national governments, which suggests why they have pushed the legislation. The FSM passed the legislation in May 2014, but then in June delayed its implementation until next year, while the Marshall Islands parliament is still debating a telecom bill.

Though it is extreme in the north Pacific nations of the FSM and Marshall Islands, where donor aid accounts for around 70 percent of government budgets, Pacific governments have become complacent and dependent on aid flow from donor countries, traditionally the U.S., Australia, Japan and New Zealand, but in recent years, Taiwan, China and the European Union have joined the mix along with donor agencies including the Asian Development Bank, World Bank and International Monetary Fund.

As times change in the world, donors are increasingly demanding results. This was not the case 40 years ago when arrangements such as the Compacts in the FSM, Marshall Islands and Palau were political vehicles to establish these three nations in close association with the U.S. and leap trusteeship termination hurdles at the United Nations. But with the political success of the Compacts and UN membership issues long since resolved, the U.S. has focused heavily on performance. Yet this has hardly been a success, something that the Australians in their new performance program should pay attention to.

Simply put, governments and aid agencies that have injected tens of millions of aid dollars into government should not expect a private sector to blossom or education standards to rise as a result of government strategic plans or new policies. Why? Because these donors are waiting and hoping for governments to initiate programs they are incapable of handling or unmotivated to maintain.

The private sector and NGOs are not, in all cases, an aid panacea. There will always be some level of corruption and poor management in these sectors as well as in government. But businesses and NGOs tend to bring vision, innovation and motivation to whatever they are doing, three elements largely missing from government programs — a fact that the new Pacific American Climate Fund is recognizing. In addition, with corruption undermining development goals and preventing benefits of aid from reaching the community, donors should consider providing resources to government audit and ombudsman offices in the region. In the Marshall Islands, for example, Auditor General Junior Patrick has attempted for going on three years to expand his office to move from a focus only on financial audits to include fraud prevention and performance audits. The fact that the Marshall Islands government and parliament continue to under-fund the Auditor General's Office, despite serious corruption in government, is another reason that performance in government isn't improving.

"We will build on what works so that funding will increasingly flow to the best performing organizations," said Minister Bishop last week. If Australia, other governments and aid agencies take an in-depth look at the region, they will see an under-funded but over-achieving NGO sector and under-capitalized private sector searching for ways to expand initiatives that produce jobs.

Why Pacific NGOs need targeted government support

These islands don't have Ford or Rockefeller Foundations waiting to provide grants to worthy organizations.

It may seem like an oxymoron to say non-government organizations should receive government funding. But in most Pacific islands, NGOs provide key community-level services yet are notoriously under-funded for the work they do. A key fact exacerbating the difficult financial situation for most NGOs is that foreign donors frequently will provide funding only for activities, but none for employees to carry out the activities.

The contribution to national development, and delivery of health, youth and women's services by NGOs around the region is obvious and irrefutable. One outstanding example is Won Smol Bag, the theater company in Vanuatu that recently celebrated its 25th anniversary of operations and now, in addition to engaging drama programs, operates health clinics, youth programs and other community activities.

Particularly in the smaller islands, though — such as Marshall Islands, Kiribati, Tuvalu, Federated States of Micronesia — there is no corporate funding base for NGOs to gain support. While businesses do contribute to NGOs, these tend to be modest few hundred-dollar donations from time to time. These islands don't have Ford or Rockefeller Foundations waiting to provide grants to worthy organizations.

NGOs, meanwhile, are driven by vision, motivation and energy — or they wouldn't exist. These attributes are, sadly, too often missing in government agencies, but fuel NGO work at the grassroots level. It is this very reason why NGOs can do impressive work and provide unmatched services to the community. And the NGOs that have operated for a decade or longer have demonstrated perseverance and, to borrow some jargon from the climate sector, "resilience" in the face of overwhelming funding challenges and odds against their continuing as going concerns. Donors repeatedly flip-flop between directly funding NGOs or channeling grants through government departments as the grant brokers, adding another layer of bureaucracy — and difficulty — for NGOs to overcome. Or international donors stop funding accomplished NGOs altogether, saying they should replace their donor aid with domestic funding. The big question, particularly for small islands, is: are there any non-government sources for core operations funding? NGOs need funding to pay staff to deliver programs, but where can they find it at home?

The irony and the impact of the vagaries of donor funding is not lost on the NGO community. Take, for example, the case of an experienced NGO outreach health worker in the Marshall Islands, whose salary was funded by donors. The staff person was dispatched to Fiji for an accredited six-month training course to upgrade her community organizing skills. When she returned to Majuro to work, she discovered funding for her salary had been eliminated by the donor agency and, despite her higher qualification and skill levels, the NGO was unable to find alternative funding. Ultimately, this skilled and experienced outreach worker migrated to the United States for work.

In the Marshall Islands, which like many island nations has an active if small NGO sector, NGOs provide a variety of skills trainings ranging from carpentry and canoe building to handicraft making and sewing, address children and youth health needs, and promote gender equality and domestic violence prevention. These areas are best served by NGOs and, in fact, are meeting important needs to which the government would otherwise have to respond. Even though government agencies such as Public Works run an occasional skills training programs and the College of the Marshall Islands offers ongoing vocational education programs, the NGOs incorporate life skills into their training programs that often make the difference between success and failure in the workplace and life in general. Waan Aelon in Majel (Canoes of the Marshall Islands), Juren Ae (loosely translated as calming or controlling the ocean current), and Youth to Youth in Health all incorporate alcohol and substance abuse counseling and numerous other life skills to make it possible for trainees who dropped out of school at an early age to successfully re-engage as productive members of their communities. In light of increasingly severe poverty in urban centers throughout the Pacific and the lack of opportunity for under-educated individuals, these NGOs are providing essential services for their islands.

But the challenge for many NGOs in the Marshall Islands and elsewhere is finding money to pay skilled staff to manage community programs. Frequently, the few paid staff in an organization end up spending most of their time chasing grants just to keep a handful of core staff on the payroll and end up with little time for program work.

Palau has established an innovative way to locally finance conservation work at the community level by devoting a portion of its high departure tax to fund conservation. Over a million dollars a year is generated to support marine and coastal conservation programs, money that can be leveraged to meet matching grants of donors.

There is no question that in the smaller islands, local communities would benefit from governments setting aside specific funding for core NGO staff — funding, for example, for a director, program manager and accountant or grants manager — that would ensure established NGOs providing community services don't disappear for lack of financing. Provision of funding for three core staff persons would give them the freedom to focus on generating grants to fund other staff and program activities. In the eight Parties to the Nauru Agreement (PNA) nations, fisheries revenue has quadrupled in recent years and is set to rise again in 2015. Setting aside $300,000 or so a year from fisheries funds to support established local NGOs — a drop in the bucket in fisheries revenue and annual budgets of most island nations — would go a long way to stabilize NGOs and ensure they are able to maintain and expand services needed by their communities. Regardless of where money comes from, targeted minimum government support of domestic NGOs will bolster the sector and encourage outside donors to match the local funding available, allowing for further expansion of health, education, business and other initiatives by NGOs.

Donors are always right, aren't they?

How helpful to overall government reform is the World Bank's policy of dangling millions of dollars in front of governments if they get rid of their telecom monopoly laws?

Donor institutions and countries can be almost as schizophrenic as the developing nations they claim they want to reform. It could be that "good governance" is simply in the eye of the beholder, not an agreed-to list of best practices that can be cloned in the same format by any government or, for that matter, donor partner.

It used to be Taiwan's and China's style of competitive diplomacy that coined the term 'checkbook' diplomacy, activity from the 1990s into the mid-2000s that saw a handful of nations globally, including several in the Pacific, flip-flopping to the highest bidder in this diplomatic game. The loans and aid — and all too often, bags of cash to politicians — didn't fit with good governance standards espoused by other donors. Until China and Taiwan settled into a comfortable rapprochement about six years ago, they were frequently the focus of criticism by other donors for lavish aid with little accountability.

Today, the Asian Development Bank, World Bank, and International Monetary Fund all promote various reforms. ADB wants governments to get their — mostly poorly run — state owned enterprises to follow models of success seen in the Solomon Islands and Samoa in recent years. World Bank is promoting competition in telecommunications, a sector long monopoly managed by government telecom outfits. IMF pushes fiscal reforms, including encouraging island countries to find ways to produce budget surpluses at year's end that can be reinvested.

But how helpful to overall government reform is the World Bank's policy of dangling millions of dollars in front of governments if they get rid of their telecom monopoly laws? For example, the Federated States of Micronesia and the Marshall Islands were offered wildly varying grants — US$43 million and US$13 million, respectively — with no strings attached for spending. The FSM was the first to pass the legislation, but then passed additional legislation holding up implementation of these same telecom changes, leaving the law in limbo. Marshalls' leaders have been embroiled in debate and legislation to liberalize the telecom sector has languished. Behind the scenes, the World Bank's International Finance Corporation is financing Digicel's expansion in the region, a fact that opponents of liberalization point out as a glaring conflict of interest. For many countries, the market is so small, there is room for only one telecom business. Should that be one financed by the World Bank, which is offering hard cash to cash-strapped governments to allow telecom competition, or of the islands' choosing, including government-run entities? That is a subject for additional comment, but the primary point is this: if competition in telecommunications will truly benefit small islands, why does World Bank need to offer a windfall of fungible cash to governments?

A key point of the ADB report, "Finding Balance 2014: Benchmarking the performance of state-owned enterprises in island countries," is that bringing the private sector into play through privatization of government operations or joint ventures can lead to success. In light of a couple of success stories in Pacific SOEs, in might behoove donors to offer some targeted money — not a free-spending grant as mentioned above — for a package of SOE reforms given their large numbers (including telecoms), significant financial losses, and large subsidies that drain government coffers.

The reality, in the meantime, is that with a few notable exceptions, governments don't want to let go of state-owned enterprises (SOEs) no matter how badly run they are or how much money they lose. The paradox, of course, is that government leaders repeatedly express their support for the private sector. For most businesses in small islands, they'd be happy with less rhetoric from government about the private sector and simply getting their bills paid by government on time. This would help the private sector immensely.

Australia and the European Union are pushing free trade agreements with the Pacific islands. Both Australia and EU provide technical and financial help so small islands can be at the negotiating table. This is all couched as "help" for small islands — paying travel costs to "negotiating sessions," hiring trade consultants to advise island governments, and so on. But, frankly, for most islands, the revenues lost in a revamp of tax laws needed to meet free trade requirements will substantially outpace the benefits of free trade with Australia, at least for the majority of smaller nations in the region. Trade "negotiations" are done in a generally collegial manner, as if to say everyone is on the same team. Who's against trade, right? But bottom line, for Australia (and New Zealand) free trade agreements are about their own national interest, just as Pacific islands should assert theirs. This has been done to a degree with the EU, as the decade long talks on an Economic Partnership Agreement broke down nearly a year ago, with government leaders walking away from the talks. Ironically, it is the Forum Secretariat — that receives large scale funding from these same donors to "facilitate" trade negotiations — that has attempted to revive the talks.

With the EU, its major interest in the region is fish. Despite this, the EU hasn't shown an inclination to accept fishing rules of the Parties to the Nauru Agreement (PNA) that many other fishing nations now accept as the new era of increasing control of the fisheries industry by Pacific islands. It should go without saying that if the EU wants access to fish in the region, it must abide by the prevailing rules, which island fisheries officials would note is simply a best-practice standard.

Interestingly, the U.S. government has ratcheted up accountability requirements for grant funding to the dismay of its long-term allies the Marshall Islands and FSM. The U.S. has taken an additional step with a new grant program for the region that avoids funding national governments altogether, a possible acknowledgment of the difficulty, from Washington, of enforcing spending rules by island governments. The Pacific American Climate Fund, launched earlier this year, states the funding is for initiatives of civil society groups and the private sector. This significant redirection of government-provided funding bears watching as it departs from the usual provision of government-to-government aid.

As the pressure for markets and resources — fish, energy, deep-sea minerals — escalates, interest in the islands will escalate. Island leaders and especially island communities need to look beyond the superficial to understand the motivation of donors. A "good governance checklist" would be a great tool for evaluating incoming grants, reforms, schemes and other plans. Sadly, such a checklist is often missing on both sides of the table.

The information age collides with older generation thinking

One of the challenges is that while there are now reams of data available on country performance in every category, political leaders in many island nations grew up in an era where decision-making based on performance indicators and information was virtually impossible.

Among Pacific island nations, the Federated States of Micronesia and the Marshall Islands rank worst and next-to-the-worst, respectively, in "ease of doing business," according to the World Bank in its latest Doing Business report for 2014.

In the UNDP's Human Development Report for 2014, only three Pacific nations rank in the 'High Human Development' category, with Palau the Pacific leader at number 60 globally. Fiji (88) and Tonga (100) are the others. Samoa, Federated States of Micronesia, Vanuatu and Kiribati make it into the "Medium Human Development" list at numbers 106, 124, 131 and 133, respectively, while Papua New Guinea and the Solomon Islands tied at 157 join mostly African nations in the "Low Human Development" list. Other island nations were not evaluated.

Three of the seven Pacific nations evaluated by the U.S. State Department for Trafficking in Persons in 2014 are on Tier 2 Watch List or Tier 3 — indicating countries that are not in compliance with minimum standards under the U.S. Trafficking Victims Protection Act (TVPA) of 2000. This includes Papua New Guinea (Tier 3) and the Marshall Islands and Solomon Islands on Tier 2 Watch List.

Of the 14 Forum island countries, only five — Cook Islands, Fiji, Niue, Palau, and Tonga — are on track to implement a majority of the seven millennium development goals by next year, according to the Pacific Islands Forum. The other nine are managing to make progress on only one or two MDGs or, as with Papua New Guinea, are off-track on all seven.

Are these reports useful to Pacific island governments? Do they contain information that should be used by individual governments as a basis for improvement?

The short answer is, 'yes.' Since performance audits tend to be few and far between, how islands are doing in development, business, trafficking, health and education are key public interest questions. Trying to outrank developed nations that are in the top 10 of various global studies is not a likely scenario for any island nation. But moving from the bottom half of a list to the top half shouldn't be out of the realm of possibility for many islands in our region.

One of the challenges is that while there are now reams of data available on country performance in every category — both from these international rankings and from domestic planning and statistics offices — political leaders in many island nations grew up in an era where there was little data available and decision-making based on performance indicators and information was virtually impossible. So decisions were made based on whatever set of assumptions leaders brought to the table.

Today, United Nations agencies and big donors in the region such as the United States, Australia and Japan are all aiming for performance, poverty reduction, and invigorating moribund economies heavily dependent on donor aid and government employment. Yet many of our decision makers discount the data being provided.

A classic example was the report for the Marshall Islands, "Juumemmej: Republic of the Marshall Islands Social and Economic Report 2005," which was attacked by the country's ruling party in parliament for bluntly talking about poverty and other social problems in the country. Despite the presentation of significant data to support its observations and recommendations, the report was largely discounted by political leaders.

Occasionally, however, governments use these performance reports to galvanize action. In the late 1990s, the Marshall Islands was placed on a global money laundering blacklist by the international Financial Action Task Force (FATF). Because of the significant harm this blacklisting had on banks and business and government operations in the country, an inter-agency group was organized to address the problem. The government brought together such entities as the Banking Commissioner, local banks, National Police, Attorney General's office, Trust Company of the Marshall Islands (which manages a ship registry and an offshore corporate registry) to deal with the FATF report. It took about two years of concerted legal work, updating laws, putting various anti-money laundering mechanisms in place, training police to investigate financial crimes, engaging with the international community on the issue, and so on. It produced a positive result: the Marshall Islands was removed from the blacklist and has stayed off because of continued engagement.

During November, a newly established government Office of

Commerce and Investment in the Marshall Islands called together government ministry and agency representatives and also local government mayors to review the World Bank's Doing Business report 2015 on the Marshall Islands. There is no reason the Marshall Islands couldn't have a better ranking in the World Bank's Doing Business report. But government legislation, policies and actions are what determine the ranking. What businesses need — Pacific wide — is not more rhetoric from government about how it supports the private sector. They need government agencies and departments to work together to streamline and improve their operations to make life easier for businesses, and put the needs of the private sector, not their government offices, as the priority.

The Office of Commerce and Investment's proactive response to the World Bank's report card on doing business in the Marshall Islands is one of the only a handful of times over recent years that the government has taken steps to address this type of performance evaluation. Often, task forces have been established by government, research conducted, reports written, recommendations submitted. And then — nothing. The reports are simply ignored and time renders them moot.

No doubt this situation is hardly unique to the Marshall Islands. Whether proactive government agencies or those in the non-government sector can get the support at the political level to make legislative and policy changes needed to improve government services and performance only time will tell as the information and performance era is up against the thinking of many politicians who are not prone to taking action based on words in a report.

'Democracy' is one word that still doesn't apply to Fiji

By Fiji's restrictive decree, which includes penalties of a fine up to $50,000 or 10 years in jail, the College of the Marshall Islands could not have sponsored its candidate debate without being subject to heavy penalty.

Fiji President Ratu Epeli Nailatikau visited the Marshall Islands, Federated States of Micronesia and Palau as part of a Pacific-region tour in the lead up to Fiji's national election in September 2014.

One of the outstanding elements of his visit to Majuro was the time he spent speaking to hundreds of high school students at the country's largest public high school about HIV/AIDS awareness. To have a person of the President's stature communicating on an important health issue brings a higher level of interest from those listening.

The visit also gave the government the opportunity to take another stab at encouraging Fiji to authorize landing rights by Air Marshall Islands/Our Airline to directly link Majuro and Tarawa in the north Pacific with Fiji in the south.

Fiji has worked diplomatically to gain support of countries in the region for its election process, and to successfully get countries such as Australia and New Zealand, which have maintained punitive sanctions on Fiji, to lift them in light of the move toward an elected parliament.

It is interesting to look at Fiji's upcoming elections through the lens of north Pacific nations and leaders, whose constitutions contain bills of rights that mirror — and in the case of the Marshall Islands are more explicit than — the Constitution of the United States, the world standard for democracy and individual rights. By these north Pacific constitutional standards, Fiji is not operating as a democracy in the lead up to the September election.

The media has been tightly controlled since soon after Commodore Voreqe Bainimarama's coup in 2006. "Since 2009, the Fiji regime's decrees, public stance and prosecutions of media owners, publishers and editors, have effectively prevented the media from being a 'watch-dog' on government," wrote Prof. Waden Narsey in 2013. "Some media organizations are now largely propaganda arms for the regime."

Fiji leadership is blunt about restricting the rights of its media and citizens to engage in election debate and discussion. The Fiji government Media Industry Development Authority recently demanded a retraction from Sean Dorney, Radio Australia's Pacific Correspondent, who at a recent Pacific media conference observed that the Fiji media isn't very free. The fact that Dorney and New Zealand journalists Michael Field and Barbara Dreaver are banned from visiting Fiji tells us how free journalists are to report on Fiji issues.

Consider also a military decree issued earlier this year for the election that states: "Following the announcement of the date of the election, it shall be unlawful for any person, entity or organization (including any person employed or engaged by any such person, entity or organization) that receives any funding or assistance from a foreign government, inter-governmental or non-governmental organization or multilateral agency to engage in, participate in or conduct any campaign (including organizing debates, public forum, meetings, interviews, panel discussions, or publishing any material) that is related to the election or any election issue or matter."

Such a decree affects not only special interest non-government organizations, but educational institutions such as the University of the South Pacific, which offer meetings (classes) on a daily basis that would by their nature discuss current events, which obviously would include the election. Such routine discussion in classrooms could easily run afoul of Fiji's regime, placing teachers, administrators and students in danger of arrest or fines, to say nothing of any specially organized debate or forum on the election.

Yet a debate or public forum is a hallmark of any free country that engages in elections and debates on the issues of the day.

Contrast that with the lead up to the Marshall Islands' national election in 2011, when the College of the Marshall Islands joined others in sponsoring a free-wheeling debate among candidates on the college's campus. By Fiji's restrictive decree, which includes penalties of a fine up to $50,000 or 10 years in jail, the College of the Marshall Islands could not have sponsored its candidate debate without being subject to heavy penalty.

It is worth quoting the bills of rights from each of the three north Pacific constitutions:

• The FSM Constitution is short and to the point: "No law may deny or impair freedom of expression, peaceable assembly, association, or petition."

• The Palau Constitution states, in part: "The government shall take no action to deny or impair the freedom of conscience or of philosophical or religious belief of any person...to deny or impair the freedom of expression or press...to deny or impair the right of any person to peacefully assemble and petition the government for redress of grievances..."

• The Marshall Islands bill of rights was similarly enacted, spelling out clearly: "Every person has the right to freedom of thought, conscience, and belief; to freedom of speech and of the press; to the free exercise of religion; to freedom of peaceful assembly and association; and to petition the government for a redress of grievances."

This section makes the important point that, while the government may impose reasonable restrictions on the time, place, or manner of conduct of peaceful assembly, any such restrictions cannot "penalize conduct on the basis of disagreement with the ideas or beliefs expressed."

Sometimes democratic rights of free speech and media run counter to traditional customs in the islands that put a premium on maintaining superficial equilibrium and discouraging confrontational activity. This is an underlying and continuous source of friction in island societies that have adopted modern constitutions while maintaining and honoring their traditional leaders and centuries old traditions.

But these constitutional freedoms are an obvious necessity for democracy to flourish in countries with modern economies and with governments making decisions involving hundreds of millions of dollars in donor aid and national revenue. My observation from visiting and living in the north Pacific for close to 40 years is that people have come to appreciate both the personal freedom their constitutions provide and the rules of governance they enshrine.

While the Marshall Islands has particular interests it is pushing as leadership cozies up to Fiji, and the FSM and Palau may also have national interests at stake in dealing with Fiji, it is impossible to avoid the conclusion that, while it is indeed welcome that Fiji has finally made the decision to hold an election, its continued muzzling of media and now NGOs in the lead up to the vote is indicative of the lack of democracy prevailing in our South Pacific neighbor.

Chapter Four: Is the Pacific Fishery Sustainable?

As tuna catch levels in the western and central Pacific soared to record volumes in the early 2010s, the Parties to the Nauru Agreement (PNA) has worked to promote greater conservation for long-term sustainability of the multi-billion dollar fishery.

Making marine protected areas succeed is no easy task

What Noah Idechong's experience and observations in Palau show is that the islands need a sea change in thinking — from fisherman to legislator — to deal with a 21st century environment that threatens to undermine coastal marine resources.

When there is attention by global media on ocean-related issues in the Pacific, it usually centers on big-time commercial fisheries: bans on shark finning, vessels arrested and fined for illegal fishing, and revenue generated by the commercial tuna fishery in the Pacific.

Rarely, however, is there media focus on local, relatively small-scale efforts to establish and maintain marine protected areas. Yet these initiatives to sustain marine resources at the village and community level in the face of pressure from commercial fishing are of huge importance to food security for communities throughout the Pacific. In fact, one might assume these local initiatives would be more enforceable than grandiose schemes such as Kiribati's Phoenix Islands Protected Area, a 150,000 square mile (388,000 square kilometers) zone, which has been criticized as a sham in a detailed recent evaluation of its implementation. It is Kiribati's protected area or shark sanctuaries declared by Palau and the Marshall Islands that grab attention of governments and media. Still, headlines don't translate to implementation and enforcement of sustainability measures at the grassroots level, where it is most needed.

The Micronesia Challenge, an initiative in the U.S.-affiliated islands north of the equator to conserve a minimum of 20 percent of land and 30 percent of coastal marine resources by 2020, has gained traction but also has a record of uneven implementation. Major global environment groups, notably Conservation International and The Nature Conservancy, have joined in making significant contributions to the Micronesian Conservation Trust in support of the Micronesian Challenge.

In the Micronesia area, Palau has the most experience in successful establishment of marine protected areas (MPAs). The past dozen years in Palau has demonstrated that local-level action by the community, NGOs and state (local) governments, must be combined with and supported by both national legislation and funding for sustainability.

One challenge is to find ways to get the attention of legislators who are buffeted by demands for funding of everything from health and education to infrastructure and transportation that they tend to ignore financing grassroots sustainability work. It is as if, because subsistence fishing and food collection is so much a part of the culture, it is taken for granted as a resource that has always been and so therefore will always be. Commercial fishing — including 'hit and run' arrangements where a company offers a local leader one-off cash in exchange for a month of harvesting clams, sea cucumbers or fish from the reef — influences unsustainable practices in all parts of the north Pacific. Even as fisheries departments try to ramp up protections and enforcement, they can be thwarted by everything from lack of legislation and enforcement personnel to bribes and unsustainable practices supported by local leaders.

Noah Idechong, a former fisheries official, founder of the Palau Conservation Society, and a former Palau National Congress House Speaker, has been involved in developing MPAs from every level in Palau. He laments the fact that people generally "don't think about the value of subsistence fishing. But if it all collapsed, how much would it take to support local communities? If we look at it this way, we can appreciate the need for sustainable harvests." What Idechong's experience and observations show is that the islands need a sea change in thinking from fisherman to legislator to deal with a 21st century environment that threatens to undermine coastal marine resources.

In 2003, Palau passed Protected Area Network (PAN) legislation that led, over time, to 12 sites around Palau meeting standards set out in the legislation. The 12 sites are eligible for funding for conservation management of the protected areas, with money coming from Palau's "green fee" — US$15 of each airport departure tax goes into a fund to support the PAN program. In 2012, US$1.8 million was generated for local-level conservation work from the nearly 120,000 visitors. The key at the community level, says Idechong, is for people to see benefit from conservation — such as employment in the community for conservation management and ranger programs. He also said NGOs and state (local) governments are not simply handed money once they qualify under the PAN designation. Money goes for management according to regulation, requiring reporting, establishment of policies and other action. He makes the point that under the legislation, communities can nominate sites, if they meet criteria they are eligible for funding, and if they do work, they receive money.

Idechong points out the usefulness of locally-generated scientific information. As part of a review several years ago of a marine protected area in Ngarchelong State, at the northern tip of Babeldaob Island in Palau, scientists discovered that 60 percent of the catch was immature fish. Palauan fishermen were following practices dating back generations, but if they continue, the science showed, it would eventually mean they'd wipe out the fish resource. Idechong and others used that information to stimulate discussion and awareness with local fishermen in Ngarchelong. He emphasized that the question asked of locals was direct: "What can *you* do about it?"

The plan, Idechong explains, is to take conservation action to the next level by moving beyond awareness of the problem to discussing closing off marine areas to rebuild the stock, and once agreement is reached on this issue, addressing how to ensure local residents have some income while an area is closed to exploitation. The aim is to get the government to provide funding while the state rebuilds its marine resources. He is hopeful that Ngarchelong will serve as an example of how a community can rebound from over-fishing in partnership with the state and national governments. In view of the Palau President Tommy Remengesau, Jr.'s environmental advocacy, the likelihood of support for this type of initiative is high.

The Marshall Islands, which over the past several years has seen the nation's fisheries department and outer island communities work to establish resource management plans and marine protected areas, has yet to pass legislation or set aside funding to make these MPAs sustainable. Idechong, on a recent visit to Majuro for discussions with Marshall Islands and Federated States of Micronesia government and environment leaders, says legislation and financing are essential to success. 'Local areas must meet criteria and funding goes to the grassroots level of the community," Idechong said. "They need a sustainable flow, even if it is small. It cannot be like a one-year grant. They need to know it will come every year so they can rely on it."

Legislation is essential to establish a system for funding and reporting, giving people confidence that money can be tracked and performance can be measured. One of the reason that donors have in recent years delivered on pledges to fund the Micronesian Conservation Trust endowment is because the MCT establishes a level of accountability and transparency that satisfies donor needs. "If donors see you making progress, they are willing to help," says Idechong. But he believes local revenue is essential to successfully implementing sustainable marine protection efforts in local communities. “It’s your house and you want to contribute before you ask for help,” he says.

The synergy that has developed among the U.S.-affiliated islands means everyone doesn’t have to reinvent the wheel for conservation work to succeed long-term. “Palau lessons can accelerate the progress in other islands,” Idechong says. “I know system are different, but the lessons are meaningful and can cut the time element for implementation.”

PNA's model should be cloned by the Pacific region

The PNA is not the only example of a functioning regional entity, but it is a leading one of how small islands can come together to generate significant benefits for their countries.

Since 2009, the Parties to the Nauru Agreement (PNA) has become a major force in the Pacific's commercial fishing industry, long dominated by distant water fishing nations. The astounding increase in revenue accruing to the eight member nations since 2010 confirms an important fact: the billions of dollars that Pacific islands have been *losing* for the past many decades by being passive sellers of licenses and operating from positions of weakness as individual nations negotiating with Japan, the United States, China, Taiwan, S. Korea and, more recently, the European Union.

In 2010, skipjack tuna caught was valued at US$1.9 billion, with only US$60 million of that going to PNA nations through licensing arrangements. By 2013, PNA CEO Dr. Transform Aqorau projects that overall fisheries revenue will increase to nearly US$3.9 billion, with the PNA share rising to US$249 million.* It's still only six percent of the revenue generated by the lucrative skipjack industry, but indicates the growing clout that this bloc of countries that control waters supplying half the world's skipjack tuna are exerting. Similarly, late last year, the U.S. government and its tuna industry agreed to pay US$63 million annually starting in 2013 for access to the PNA area, up from US$21 million a year.

The PNA area encompasses the Marshall Islands, Kiribati, Tuvalu, Nauru, Federated States of Micronesia, Palau, Solomon Islands and Papua New Guinea.

PNA has not only more than tripled revenue from fisheries, it has driven conservation management initiatives ranging from annual moratoriums on use of fish aggregation devices (FADs) to banning fishing in high seas pockets adjacent to PNA nations' 200-mile exclusive economic zones. The management control it is exerting is allowing it to develop business initiatives to bring greater domestic investment in fisheries and to create value-added products, such as sustainably caught tuna that are harvested without the use of FADs. The Marine Stewardship Council recently certified PNA's skipjack fishery. Fish caught without FADs will carry the MSC certification symbol, which is expected to command higher value in the European and U.S. markets where consumers will pay more for sustainably caught tuna.

Does the PNA model have application elsewhere in the region? Absolutely. But the problem is old style, bad governance exists at many levels of government throughout the region. So why should politicians who see government as their own private business, to be exploited for personal benefit, use the PNA model in other areas?

There is pressure from commercial interests outside the region to get access for marine resources, deep-sea mining, and land resources. It is really easy for island leaders — mayors, governors, members of parliament, high-ranking landowners — to fall prey to outside interests. Despite its membership in PNA, the Marshall Islands, for example, sees local governments willing to sign off on deals with Asian fishing companies through agreements that would not pass a "good governance" test. The recent granting by the Vanuatu government of licenses to deep-sea mining interests prompted community opposition for its lack of transparency.

The fact is, there are plenty of outsiders looking to cash in by exploiting island resources for a fraction of what they're worth — the Pacific tuna fishery is a prime example. Money aside, what is worse is that without conservation rules to govern the exploitation, at the local level, small island communities can wake up one morning to find their source of subsistence wiped out for a few thousand dollars that was handed to their leaders.

The challenges PNA has had to overcome in forcing conservation measures on the fleets of distant water fishing nations shows that without entities such as PNA, these outside industries would exploit the fishery until it is wiped out — following similar patterns globally that have seen the collapse of other commercial fisheries.

In the Pacific, we frequently see island leaders willing to engage in ad hoc, one-off deals with outside companies for quick money. Sadly, as the tuna fishery shows, without a focused, coordinated and informed approach to doing business with Asians, Europeans, Americans, Australians and others, most Pacific islanders get the short end of the stick. This could be explained away many years ago by lack of communication, which meant people in one island had no clue about what was happening in a neighboring country, nor access to examples of "best practice" that could be applied.

But the Internet, regional organizations, and frequent meetings in the Pacific means there is no reason — other than blatant corruption — for leaders to keep doing the one-off, ad hoc deals that are detrimental to local communities and sometimes their country as a whole. The PNA is not the only example of a functioning regional entity, but it is a leading example of how small islands can come together to generate significant benefits for their countries.

Still, demonstrating how hard it is to maintain this type of unity across borders, the PNA itself has its own share of flashpoints. In 2012, Kiribati refused to abide by fishing day limits, prompting a reprimand from the other countries and a promise that it would not break ranks this year. The division of the approximately 45,000 fishing days among the eight PNA member nations causes disputes, though none that to date have risen to the point of breaking up the PNA. But there are countries ready and willing to ignore PNA rules if one of its members is willing to negotiate directly with it — another confirmation of the difficulty in getting good governance principles embedded in dealings with foreign commercial interests, even when the template is in use by the country in question.

No multi-national organization is conflict free, and PNA is no exception. It has shown, however, that the old axiom "unity is strength" is a fact that is benefiting Pacific islands like never before.

* In 2015, the estimated revenue accruing to the eight PNA member nations from the vessel day scheme was expected to rise above US$350 million, a five-fold increase since 2010.

The battle comes to the Western and Central Pacific Fisheries Commission

'If distant water fishing nations support sustainability of the resource, then they need to commit to a 30 percent reduction in catches. They have to do it or face the consequences.'

Is the huge amount of money being made by the tuna industry in the Pacific a disincentive to getting distant water fishing nations to agree to aggressive conservation measures that ensure the long-term sustainability of the fishery? It appears so.

The tuna catch in the Pacific set a record in 2012, both in value — US$7 billion — and in volume — 2.65 million tons. But scientists have warned for several years that bigeye tuna is being overfished and yellowfin tuna is at its maximum level of sustainable exploitation. The message is clear: reductions in effort, meaning fewer boats, and cutbacks in tonnage caught must be implemented to ensure the Pacific's tuna fishery remains vibrant for years to come.

The annual meeting of the Western and Central Pacific Fisheries Commission (WCPFC) opens in Cairns, Australia in December 2013 and by all expectations, it will a showdown between island members of the Forum Fisheries Agency (FFA) and some distant water fishing nations.

According to FFA Deputy Director Wez Norris, since earlier in the year when Japan, the Philippines and the eight island members of the Parties to the Nauru Agreement (PNA) endorsed a joint conservation proposal to be put to the WCPFC meeting next week, positions on catch reductions and conservation measures have "polarized and have moved apart." This 10-nation "joint proposal" is a "viable way for the WCPFC to achieve substantial reductions in bigeye over-fishing in a way that does not shoulder a disproportionate burden onto small island developing states (SIDS) and sets up avenues for more equitable fisheries management in the long term," Norris points out. "All FFA members have agreed to support the proposal as a way forward so there is a high degree of agreement going into the meeting."

The problem, however, is substantial opposition from a number of the developed nation members of the WCPFC. The WCPFC has 25 members, including the European Union as a group, and operates by consensus. Those countries opposing the joint measure from

PNA, Japan and Philippines are among the primary beneficiaries of the bigeye fishery but want management measures that will minimize impact on their longline fleets while placing additional conservation burdens on fisheries that occur in the exclusive economic zones (EEZs) of Pacific nations.

For example, FFA members have been calling for additional longline management for several years. There has been opposition from the major fleets that this management would apply to, and a strong tendency for them to push the onus of bigeye conservation onto the purse seine fishery. Norris makes the point that while "it is unquestionable that the purse seine fishery must contribute to conservation, it simply cannot do so alone." He also points out that FFA members are flexible, but want to see alternative proposals for action if theirs are not supported by the distant water fleet.

"For the current proposal to have any prospect for agreement, there will need to be a genuine spirit of compromise and negotiation," says Norris. "FFA members will be looking to other developed countries to follow the lead that Japan has set in moving away from traditional positions and seeking arrangements that will work." But with world market tuna prices over US$2,000 a ton in 2013 — more than double what they were just several years ago — there is more pressure than ever on tuna stocks by the fishing industry.

The joint tuna conservation proposal focuses on bigeye, yellowfin and skipjack tuna. Recommendations on the table next week include reducing the catch of bigeye by longliners by 45 percent of 2004 levels by 2017, and for skipjack, to expand an annual ban on use of fish aggregation devices (FADs) by purse seiners from the current three months to four months starting in 2014 and to five months beginning in 2017. In addition to conservation measures in the 200-mile exclusive economic zones of PNA nations, it seeks to cap the number of fishing days allowed annually on the high seas.

Executive Director of the WCPFC Glenn Hurry warned Forum island leaders in September 2013 about the urgent need for fisheries management action. Despite scientific evidence that bigeye tuna is being over-fished, Hurry said the WCPFC has been unable to get agreement from its membership to reduce bigeye catches. Hurry said the number of vessels fishing for tuna continue to increase in the Pacific, with last year's 297 purse seiners setting an all-time high — and more are being built. The increasing number of vessels will "cause sustainability problems in the fishery," he said. "What we now see from the 2012 fishing data is more boats in the fishery, higher overall catches, smaller fish sizes, and the lowest ever levels of fisheries biomass for these tuna stocks."

Marshall Islands fisheries Director Glen Joseph told me the situation is worse even than Hurry's comments suggest. "It's not just bigeye tuna raising concern," he said. "Swordfish catches are raising a red flag." And yellowfin tuna is reported by scientists to be at its maximum sustainable yield. "If distant water fishing nations support sustainability of the resource, then they need to commit to a 30 percent reduction in catches," Joseph said. "It's not a question of should they do it or not. They have to do it or face the consequences."*

Some observers see a disturbing trend at recent WCPFC annual meetings with the focus of discussions shifting from the high seas, which the Commission was established to manage, to in-zone, which is the jurisdiction of the individual FFA members. Joseph says this has derailed urgently needed implementation of fishing rules on the high seas — the area that is under jurisdiction of the WCPFC. "There has been a major effort at conservation and management in-zone," said Joseph. "But less so on the high seas."

In-zone measures, such as those put forward by PNA, often get the most debate at WCPFC meetings because the islands are actively working to conserve the resource. "But the Commission should be focused on the high seas and it starts from the provision of catch and effort data," Joseph said, adding that for seven year most of the distant water fishing nations have not delivered on a promise to provide catch data from high seas fishing. "Coastal states are trying to comply (with WCPFC rules). We're developing monitoring, control and surveillance measures to enforce rules, we are participating in the regional observer program, and we are providing catch and effort data."

But, said Joseph, the islands' management measures "become the subject of scrutiny and debate at Commission meetings and the high seas gets left off the agenda."

As the 2013 annual WCPFC meeting approaches, Joseph said PNA and coastal states "have to be optimistic (about the Commission taking action) because we have something on the table. We have to capitalize on it. If our measure is rejected, it will be a rejection by distant water fishing nations of coastal states' interests and a breach of the WCPFC treaty's Article 30 (which requires the WCPFC to 'give full recognition to the special requirements of developing states parties to this Convention, in particular small island developing states')."

Norris notes that an agreement "is certainly possible and the proposal on the table provides an excellent platform for discussion.

But it requires all members to act positively, proactively, cooperatively and with a long-term view."

There is precedent for WCPFC to affirm conservation measures. In 2008, PNA members agreed to enforce a series of measures for their own EEZ —three-month moratorium on using fish aggregation devices (FADs) annually, a halt to fishing in high seas "pockets" as a license requirement to fish in EEZs, use of a new "vessel day scheme" — and then took these to the WCPFC. Norris explains that the WCPFC "did the right thing and introduced compatible measures in other areas and complemented that with longline management. It was an excellent outcome and one that sadly did not get the praise it deserved."

But what started out as a strong set of measures supporting sustainable fishing has been revised twice by WCPFC membership since 2008 such that the balance has shifted away from the interests of many FFA members. 'High seas management has been substantially weakened, control and authority of purse seine measures have been vested in flag states, even when operating in EEZs, closures have been removed and there has been no additional longline management, said Norris. 'Time is running short for the WCPFC as a whole to demonstrate that it is capable of breaking new ground, as it did in 2008 and finalizing an agreement that will last more than 12 months.

Failure on the part of the WCPFC to adopt strong conservation measures that include a reduction in tuna catches will simply embolden the islands to adopt their own measures that will cover the majority of the fishery. A lack of action by the WCPFC will undermine its role as a credible regional fisheries management organization, particularly if island nations see they cannot get collaborative action from distant water fishing nations to support sustainability of the resource.

Commission Executive Director Hurry issued an ultimatum recently. All Commission members, including Forum islands, "must demonstrate this year that they are capable of taking hard decisions for the management of the region's tuna stocks," Hurry said. "These decisions will mean reduced levels of catch for bigeye tuna, it will mean agreeing to management arrangements for the catch of yellowfin and skipjack tuna, and it will mean capping and reducing the number of vessels in the fishery."

"If we as coastal nations want to sustain the resource for the next 50 years," said Joseph, "we must insist on a 30 percent reduction in effort and mortality by key tuna species of concern."

These are decisions that cannot continue to be delayed. But at both the 2013 and 2014 annual meetings of the WCPFC, the Commission failed to adopt measures to reduce bigeye tuna catches to the extent called for by scientists and island nations.

Greed trumps conservation in the Pacific

'We're trying to tell people: you can't fish at this level and expect it to last.'

So much money is being made from the Western and Central Pacific tuna fishery that virtually no one wants to heed the message of scientists and managers whose conservation advice is falling on deaf ears. With the emergence of the Parties to the Nauru Agreement (PNA) as a major player in the region since 2010 and enforcement of its "vessel day scheme," tuna revenues accruing to the eight PNA member nations have quadrupled — and is set to rise again in 2015, when the minimum fishing day fee jumps from the current US$6,000 to US$8,000.

But before we start feeling sorry for a fishing industry that is now paying four times or more than in the past to access the PNA's rich fishing waters, consider that in 2012 the estimated total tuna tonnage caught set a record of 2.6 million tons, generating revenue in the neighborhood of US$4 billion. Skipjack tuna prices on the world market set an all-time high of US$2,300 a ton in mid-2013, and though the price plummeted from over-supply late last year and remained low earlier this year (2014), it is heading back up and is in the US$1,500 level as of July.

It's big money. In some islands, the revenue flowing from fisheries accounts for as much as a third to half of locally-generated funds for national governments. With the number of purse seiners rising from 226 in 2000 to over 300 this year, it's obvious that the industry is cashing in, too.

"If we want a train wreck instead of a sustainable fishery, we should keep going the way we are now," warned Glenn Hurry, the outgoing Executive Director of the Western and Central Pacific Fisheries Commission (WCPFC).

Fisheries scientists will release results of a three-year Pacific tuna stock assessment in August 2014. Hurry says the results are expected to confirm what scientists have been saying in recent years: Bigeye tuna is on the brink of being over-fished and measures adopted over the past six years to reduce catch levels have not worked; yellowfin tuna is likely at its maximum sustainable fishing level and the region could be in danger of seeing significantly reduced stock levels if ongoing heavy fishing continues unabated; and skipjack tuna, though still at healthy stock levels, is now at about 50 percent of its original biomass.

The fishery is seeing an increase in the number of boats and improved sophistication of catch technology — everything from fish aggregation devices that have tuna-tracking sonar to larger vessels with greater capacity — that add up to greatly increased pressure on the resource.

"The news isn't good and no one wants to hear it," says Hurry, who left his post in August, 2014 after four years at the head of the Pohnpei-based WCPFC. "We're trying to tell people: you can't fish at this level and expect it to last."

Pacific islands and the PNA nations in particular — Papua New Guinea, Kiribati, Federated States of Micronesia, Solomon Islands, Nauru, Tuvalu, Marshall Islands and Palau — have the greatest interest in sustaining stocks and the ability to cap, and reduce, fishing effort in the region. But as the cash rolls into government coffers from the industry, it may get increasingly difficult to reduce fishing effort. In 2012, for example, despite the PNA members agreeing to a specific number of fishing days for each member, Kiribati continued to sell days over and above its limit. It is no secret, either, that other PNA members have skillfully managed grey areas, such as so-called "non-fishing days," to their and the industry's benefit.

And many islands now have domestic fleets of fishing vessels — either joint venture with foreign fishing companies, wholly owned, or locally flagged — that they are promoting to gain more benefits from the industry.

Simply put, the more valuable the industry gets to the islands, the more difficult it will be to reduce catch levels and the number of fishing vessels at work in the Pacific.

PNA set 44,623 as the limit for fishing days in 2014 and 2015. A number of PNA members are expected to exhaust their allotted share of days before the end of year, a development that under PNA rules will require them to close their EEZs to fishing. The Solomon Islands and other countries have closed their EEZs to fishing in recent years when they ran out of days — action that is a 'best practice' because it both conserves the resource and increases the value of days, but is nevertheless difficult to do because of money to be made by selling more days.

One important mechanism for maintaining PNA-established fishing day limits is PNA's trading scheme. The concept is that if one member sells all its fishing days, it can buy days off other members so that fishing can continue in their zones. If migratory tuna are not in the waters of the Marshall Islands, for example, it may not be able to sell all of its fishing days. If tuna fishing is heavy in, for example, PNG and the Solomon Islands, they may need additional days so that fishing can continue. By purchasing days from members who have them, PNA can remain within its overall fishing day limit, while maintaining value through the trading system for members whose zones are not being fished. The fishing day trading system has been used on and off over the past three years, and clearly has an important future role if overall fishing limits are to be maintained.

Still, history is not on the Pacific's side. Throughout the world, one fishery after another has crashed, throwing fishermen out of jobs and causing economic chaos as well as loss of important food sources.

Knowledge is power, but can it trump increasing fisheries revenue? That is the key challenge facing the Pacific islands today as they attempt to both control and gain more benefit from the lucrative tuna fishery.

Unity is paying off in the Pacific — at least in fisheries

The fact that distant water fishing nations had to be forced by the PNA, FFA and the Tuna Commission to comply with changes to sustain and stabilize the industry simply underlines the point that unity works.

As Pacific islands ratchet up control of fishing in their waters, we've seen a predictable response from distant water fishing nations.

When the Western and Central Pacific Fisheries Commission (also known as the "Tuna Commission") was established by treaty 10 years ago, the Japanese government, despite its active participation in negotiations leading up to the treaty, refused to sign on at the first opportunity. Despite being part of the negotiations, it said it wouldn't back the newly established regional fisheries management organization for the Pacific. Was it unsurprising that a year later, Japan signed on?

The Parties to the Nauru Agreement (PNA), which has set itself up as a fisheries cartel, established a vessel day scheme for selling fishing days, with the goal of limiting the then-uncontrolled level of purse seine fishing to conserve tuna and increase its value. PNA has certainly been successful in the latter (tuna revenue flowing to the eight member nations has risen from US$60 million annually in 2010 to over US$250 million in 2013), if not as successful at the former.

But when PNA started enforcing the vessel day scheme, most distant water fishing nations balked at accepting it. They had been used to sending fisheries teams to island capitals once a year to negotiate license fees, which historically paid just pennies compared to the profits reaped by the fishing countries. These countries were not about to change a style of operation that had fed their fishing industries for two generations. Now, with the exception of the European Union, all distant water fishing nations with purse seiners operating in the region are fishing under the vessel day scheme. Shall we take bets on the EU's ultimate acquiescence to the vessel day scheme?

Then there are the Americans, who have enjoyed preferential access to PNA waters since the late 1980s, when a U.S. State Department-backed fishing treaty came into play with all Forum

Fisheries Agency islands. The treaty ended years of U.S. flagged boats fishing without paying, ignoring rules, and generally giving the U.S. a bad name in the region. When the treaty's financial package came up for renegotiation several years ago, the U.S. was paying US$21 million annually. The PNA demanded triple this amount. "It's too much," said U.S. negotiators. "We can't pay it." Over the ensuing years of negotiation the U.S. side finally agreed to pay $63 million a year, a deal that went through in 2013. Now PNA has upped the access ante because it is increasing the fishing day fee from US$6,000 to US$8,000 come January 1, 2015. And the U.S. has tentatively agreed to US$87 million a year to secure fishing access for it vessels. "Can't afford it?" The better question is, "do you want to keep fishing?" And the U.S. government and industry clearly know the answer to this question.

With it now clear that bigeye tuna are being over-fished, the move for greater control of the longline fishing industry is gaining momentum. Since the 3,000 longliners plying the Pacific generally fish on the high seas, they are more difficult to manage than the purse seiners that fish "in-zone." Still, PNA has announced plans to extend a vessel day scheme to longliners to bring it under the control and management of Pacific islands.

As pointed out last week at a fisheries meeting by Phil Roberts, the managing director of global tuna supply company Tri-Marine International, "When PNA banned high seas transshipment for purse seiners, there were some grips. But then everyone started doing in-port transshipment." In-port transshipment meets dual conservation and economic development goals for Pacific islands: it increased the opportunity for monitoring vessel catches, while offering numerous spinoff economic benefits to Pacific ports. One of the key proposals on the table is to halt longliners transshipping on the high seas, which is where virtually all of the distant water fishing fleet currently off-loads its catches of tuna — a system that is problematic for effective fisheries management and producing accurate stock assessments.

The longline industry of Japan, S. Korea, Taiwan and China is not helping matters, either. The fact that these four nations have, since the start of Tuna Commission a decade ago, failed to provide operational catch data that is a requirement of membership appears finally to be coming to a head. The 17-member Forum Fisheries Agency (FFA) issued a strongly worded statement in August calling for action by these four nations to provide data to reduce gaps in stock assessments. An increasing number of Pacific fisheries officials want the Tuna Commission to sanction these countries for failure to provide the required data.

History tells us that if island countries stay unified, they can gain control over an industry long dominated by distant water fishing nations. Enforcing "best practice" management rules is the only way to ensure the future viability of tuna stocks not only for Pacific islanders, who depend on this for food security, government services and jobs, but for the rest of the world that is increasingly dependent on tuna fish as a food source. The fact that distant water fishing nations have had to be forced, sometimes kicking and screaming, by the PNA, FFA and the Tuna Commission to comply with changes to sustain and stabilize the industry, while sharing the benefit with island nations, simply underlines the point that unity works.

The PNA and FFA have proved over the years that there is power in numbers. It's an example of success for the region that could easily be applied to other economic areas, including deep-sea mining.

Tuna sustainability is a huge economic issue for the Pacific

The extent to which the PNA will go to limit and in some cases reduce tuna fishing in the Pacific may surprise distant water fishing nations.

The Western and Central Pacific Fisheries Commission (WCPFC) annual meeting opens in Apia, Samoa December 1, 2014 with an agenda that is critically important to the sustainability of the region's tuna industry — valued at over US$6 billion in 2013. In light of the growing dependence of the economies of many island nations on the tuna industry, finding a way to sustain the resource in a tuna-hungry world goes to the heart of sustainability of island employment, national budgets, tax revenues, and government services.

The Parties to the Nauru Agreement (PNA) group are going to be the leading force pushing for ramped up rules to prevent overfishing of tuna in the region at next week's meeting. But will they be successful in the face of a fishing industry reluctant to change?

Just as PNA-member Kiribati shocked the United States purse seine fishing industry in early October 2014 when it announced it would not provide thousands of fishing days to U.S. vessels as it had in the past, the extent to which the PNA will go to limit and in some cases reduce tuna fishing in the Pacific may surprise distant water fishing nations. What it comes down to is Pacific islands taking control of the tuna resource and forcing the industry, long controlled by distant water nations, to follow the rules laid down by the islands.

Many people in PNA are less than optimistic about the chances of getting the WCPFC to take decisive action next week in light of its inability to do so the past several years. "Looking ahead, PNA members will likely need to reassess their approach to bigeye conservation and management if our measure is not approved at WCPFC 11 in Samoa in light of the burden of bigeye conservation and management being placed on small island developing states through the current conservation and management measure," said Dr. Transform Aqorau, CEO of the PNA, last week. His point: the

PNA have already ratcheted up conservation measures in their 200-mile zones — limiting the use of fish aggregation devices, for example — but the WCPFC has not followed suit for the high seas, where most of the longliners, which target bigeye tuna, are fishing.

Pacific islands and distant water fishing nations have been put on notice by the latest regional stock assessment that catches, particularly for bigeye, a tuna coveted by the Asian, American and European sashimi market, must be capped or reduced. The scientists recommended a reduction in bigeye tuna fishing, no increase in catch levels for yellowfin tuna, and setting limits on fishing for skipjack tuna to maintain stocks at current healthy levels. But none of this is doable if the WCPFC fails to act.

The Parties to the Nauru Agreement have put a detailed plan of action on the table that aims to reel in largely out-of-control longline fishing on the high seas and to reduce the use of "fish aggregation devices" — or FADs — that lead to large catches of juvenile bigeye.

But the Fisheries Commission has failed to take decisive action in the past several annual meetings. PNA and Forum Fisheries Agency islands are becoming increasingly disillusioned with the unwillingness of distant water fishing nations to agree to needed cutbacks in fishing for bigeye, as well as limiting catches of yellowfin and skipjack tuna.

And they are showing this by turning the industry on its head. Despite an historic US$90 million one-year fisheries deal reached in Honolulu in October 2014, all sides say the Pacific's long-term treaty with the United States must be redrawn. This fisheries deal sparked much media reporting and comment, especially when Kiribati announced it was going to provide only a fraction of the fishing days the U.S. fleet was seeking. Why is Kiribati not providing days to the U.S. fleet through the treaty? It's about business.

During a late-2014 negotiating session between the U.S. and the 17 island nations that benefit from the U.S. treaty, the U.S. was shocked to hear Kiribati say it would offer only 300 days for U.S. vessels to use under the treaty — after providing several thousand days annually in recent years. But the U.S. shouldn't have been surprised by this latest development. It's been in the offing since 2010.

While leaders from the Forum island countries have said they want their fisheries officials to extend the treaty with the U.S., PNA nations are less than enthusiastic. Why? Because under the treaty, a price is locked in for U.S. access to fishing days that, in the view of PNA countries, undervalues the days. Many PNA countries don't like being locked into providing days to the U.S. treaty — which requires 8,000 fishing days per year in PNA waters — because they can usually sell those days to other fleets for more money. While the minimum price of a fishing day in 2014 has been US$6,000, we've seen days sell for as high as US$13,000 because of heavy demand. In October, virtually all days for the year were sold and fishing companies were scrambling to buy or trade a few more days to continue fishing until the end of the year — a situation that puts a financial premium on days, to the benefit of the islands. But under the U.S. treaty, a price is locked in for the year: the Forum Fisheries Agency gets a management fee for administering the treaty, 15 percent is split equally among all 17 islands, and a few other deductions reduce what is left to pay the islands where U.S. purse seiners actually catch the fish.

With most of the fishing the past two years focused in Kiribati's vast EEZ, Kiribati knows it can command a premium price because virtually all fleets want to fish in their waters. According to PNA, Kiribati's message to the U.S. is not "don't fish in our waters." Instead, Kiribati wants to sell days bilaterally to the U.S. — outside of the treaty — as it does with other fleets so it can control the price.

Another development that has turned the industry upside down is Papua New Guinea's National Fisheries Authority's successful public tender of fishing days conducted in late 2014. Although the minimum price for fishing days in 2015 is US$8,000, through the tender, PNG gained payment as high as US$12,000 per day. Through the public tender, PNG restructured the number of days allocated to domestic and distant water fishing nation vessels, and addressed the ongoing problem that offloading tuna for domestic processing has not kept pace with requirements for distant water vessels or concessions provided to domestic vessels.

The tender put distant water fishing nations on notice that compliance with agreements that require vessels to land fish for processing will be enforced, pointing out that despite fishing access agreements requiring fishing boats to land 10 percent of their catches in PNG, "not one fish has ever been landed for processing."

The actions of both Kiribati and PNG have been made possible by the PNA's "vessel day scheme" (VDS) that allocates a certain number of fishing days for the year to each member country and establishes a minimum day price. That price has skyrocketed with tuna revenues accruing to PNA members quadrupling, showing how the VDS has allowed PNA to shape the industry over the past five years.

In Apia, PNA faces its greatest challenge: Gaining agreement of distant water fishing nations to reduce mortality of bigeye tuna by reducing catches of longliners and most importantly, getting the Asian longline industry to provide operational catch data that for 10 years it has refused to give to the WCPFC, despite it being an obligation of membership. PNA is calling for catch levels to be cut further for nations that continue to avoid providing operational catch data — which is essential to estimating the total harvest every year and to producing accurate stock assessments.

Bigeye tuna is on the edge of an abyss, and whether it continues to be a billion dollar global industry will be determined by actions taken by islands and distant water fishing nations to reduce catches of both longliners and purse seiners. If these actions don't come about next week in Apia, the PNA will be forced to do what it has in the past: make rules for high seas tuna conservation that are a condition for fishing in PNA zones.

Chapter Five: Climate takes Center Stage in the Pacific

Annual king tides coupled with storm surges have produced increasingly frequent saltwater inundations in atolls, including this graveyard located along an ocean side shoreline in Majuro Atoll, capital of the Marshall Islands.
Photo: Suzanne Chutaro.

What is the best way to engage diplomatic partners in climate action?

'We feel very strongly that if (Secretary of State Kerry) does not attend it would be a slap in the face and like the United States would be reversing its so-called pivot to the Pacific.'

The aggressive campaign of the Marshall Islands to gain global action on climate change comes against a backdrop of increasingly worrying scientific reports about the evolving threat of rising sea levels. The hosting in September 2013 of the Pacific Islands Forum by the Marshall Islands activated government leadership as never before on the climate issue. They ramped up rhetoric and the country's media profile to full wattage, with campaigns focusing on the United States and Australia, calling on their leaders take the lead by joining Pacific countries to avert a climate catastrophe.

Clearly, if the Forum wants the world to take a climate leadership pitch seriously, it needs the U.S., Australia and Japan — all of which have to some degree acknowledged the developing climate crisis. So the real question is how to bring the leaders of these nations along. That question in so far as Australia goes won't be answerable until after the September 7, 2013 election, which falls the day after the end of the Forum in Majuro, ensuring that Foreign Minister Bob Carr will attend the Majuro meetings instead of PM Kevin Rudd.

As to the United States, when the Marshall Islands' host government did not receive confirmation of its invitation earlier in the year for U.S. Secretary of State John Kerry to attend the Forum in Majuro, it went on a media blitz in July. In the widely read U.S.-based Huffington Post, President Christopher Loeak, in a blog, issued an open letter to Kerry in late July, publicly inviting the Secretary to come to Majuro to launch a "new wave of political momentum to tackle the challenge of our generation." The President said the Marshall Islands wanted Kerry in Majuro so he could show the U.S. government's support for a "Majuro Declaration for Climate Leadership."

Minister in Assistance to the President Tony deBrum followed this up with a high-profile week in Australia, speaking on climate change to government officials, university and donor groups, and the media. The Australian newspaper The Age headlined, "Marshall Islands urges its 'big brother' to stand up for it on climate change," a story about deBrum calling for the Australian government to step up its climate engagement. He also said Secretary Kerry needed to be at the Forum in Majuro. "We feel very strongly that if (Kerry) does not attend it would be a slap in the face and like the United States would be reversing its so-called pivot to the Pacific," deBrum said.*

Although Pacific islands will be among the first to suffer the effects of climate change, with the possible exception of Papua New Guinea, island countries and territories are so miniscule in the global context as to be off the map. The Forum as a unified group can attract greater traction in international meetings on climate change, but it clearly needs at least a couple of the developed Pacific rim nations to lend weight to whatever declaration is issued in Majuro.

For governments that need the U.S., Australia and Japan on board on this issue and have the diplomatic connections to gain face-to-face, closed door meetings with the highest levels in these three governments, it would seem that the Marshall Islands, if not the Forum, is wasting capital with its recent publicity barrage. The rhetoric resonates well with other Forum island countries that are in the same boat, but that is preaching to the converted. In light of business, public and government sentiment in developed countries that are hurdles to climate action, getting some of the Pacific's key donor partners to demonstrate leadership on climate change is a huge undertaking that will take quiet but persistent diplomatic engagement combined with, at strategic points, publicity campaigns.

The Majuro Forum's theme, "Marshalling a Pacific Response to the Climate Challenge," will keep the issue front and center in Majuro, and is expected to result in a stand alone declaration calling for global leadership to avoid a climate catastrophe.**

Besides promoting a draft of the proposed climate change declaration among Forum members in the lead up to the September 3-6, 2013 leaders meeting, the Marshall Islands is sponsoring a special panel of experts' roundtable on climate leadership on the Forum theme the day before the official opening. Officials representing a variety of institutions working on climate change issues are flying into Majuro to offer presentations at this half-day event, which is timed to gain media exposure the day prior to the official opening of the Forum.

The aim is to use a Majuro climate change declaration to jump start expanding regional leadership efforts for next year's Third International Conference on Small Island Developing States to be held in Samoa in September 2014, and a summit of world leaders on climate that UN Secretary General Ban-ki Moon is sponsoring in 2014.***

Pacific nations have little clout in global climate change negotiations, but it would appear that a clear statement will come out of Majuro calling on developed nations for action far beyond what we've seen to date to reduce greenhouse gas emissions to avert a worst-case climate scenario. A key issue at this point is getting Pacific rim nations that are already engaged in the Pacific to endorse a Majuro declaration of action to help propel it onto the global agenda.

** Secretary of State Kerry did not attend the 2013 Pacific Islands Forum in Majuro. Instead, Interior Secretary Sally Jewell led the U.S. delegation. Her attendance was described by Marshall Islands Foreign Minister Phillip Muller as "very disappointing," and "a slap in the face." Kerry did, however, appear in a special climate-related video produced for a Forum session in Majuro on climate action.*

*** The 2013 Pacific Islands Forum endorsed the Majuro Declaration for climate leadership. Subsequently, the United States and a number of other nations joined the declaration.*

**** The UN Climate Summit 2014 featured Marshallese poet Kathy Jetnil-Kijiner who sparked a rare standing ovation from heads of state in the General Assembly hall for her presentation of a poem to her infant daughter about the climate threat, "Dear Matafele Peinam." Her performance can be viewed on YouTube.*

Do Pacific islands need to make domestic changes while campaigning globally?

'I've seen some sections of islands erode over a hundred feet, yet other nearby sections are completely stable.'

Marshall Islanders living on low-lying windward coastlines were shocked awake in the early morning hours of March 3, 2014 when storm surges drove king tide waves into their homes and across roads. Nearly a thousand people were left temporarily homeless in Majuro, as the high tide demolished or damaged dozens of houses, dumping rocks, coral, garbage and other debris in people's homes and yards, and across the roads.

It was the third high tide to inundate sections of Majuro since February 2013. "While king tides are not new to the Marshall Islands, their frequency and ferocity are clearly intensifying," said Foreign Minister Phillip Muller. "For those of us in the Pacific, silly discussions about the scientific truth of climate change are futile. We see with our own eyes that the oceans are rising, and our tide gauges confirm it. We know there is only one explanation for this unprecedented phenomenon — climate change has arrived."

In March 2014, the American Association for the Advancement of Science released a plainspoken report to alert the public to the facts of the climate crisis. "Human-caused climate change is happening, we face risks of abrupt, unpredictable and potentially irreversible changes, and responding now will lower the risk and cost of taking action," said the report. The AAAS made the point that 97 percent of all scientists agree that human-caused climate change is a reality.

Leaders from the Marshall Islands in the past couple of years have joined leaders from Kiribati, Tuvalu and the Maldives in speaking international to gain global recognition about climate change and impacts of rising sea levels. If we need more evidence, the Australian government-installed tidal monitoring equipment in Majuro and other locations around the western Pacific now provides a 20-year snapshot confirming that the sea level is indeed rising in the region.

What does this mean for residents of atolls and low-lying areas such as the Rewa Delta in Fiji? And more importantly, what does it mean for governments, which must respond to frequent flooding and consequent damage?

In 2009, University of the South Pacific Suva-based climate researcher Dr. Patrick Nunn said islands should begin talking about relocation now to be prepared for the impact of rising sea levels 25 years from now. His comment underscores a point about government preparation, raising the issue: what should governments be doing domestically in addition to campaigning globally for action to mitigate climate change?

One of the modern-day realities in the Pacific is overcrowded urban centers. As people migrate into the cities, the crowding puts more people at risk when floods or major storms hit the islands, exacerbating pressure on government services.

As demand for land in the urban centers grows, people build on ever more marginal pieces of property. Prior to World War II, most of Majuro's small population lived on the largest island at the western end of the atoll. Only a handful of people lived in what is now the "downtown" section, a three-mile strip of land now home to an estimated 20,000 people. No zoning is enforced, which allows people to build anywhere a landowner authorizes a dwelling to be located. Many plywood and tin roof houses, some little more than shacks, have been constructed literally a meter or less from the high tide mark. It's the reality of urban living in islands such as Majuro and Tarawa in Kiribati. Based on past experience, local residents know where the most likely flood zones will be when there is an extra high tide.

The question this raises is, in light of three flooding incidents that caused damage in Majuro and several populated outer islands in 2013-2014 requiring government emergency action, is the government going to continue responding to these emergency situations as one-off incidents? Can they be planned for, and if so how?

An obvious idea is where and how people construct homes. The use of stilts would seem to be a useful step, not only as a flood response mechanism, but also to improve energy efficiency of homes. The "where" is more difficult in the Marshalls because all land is privately owned and local governments have been reluctant to enforce zoning standards. This has led to numerous areas of fire hazard because, in many cases, roofs are touching or less than a meter apart. It has also allowed people to build in areas that repeatedly flood. While it is more difficult to do, another course of action is to alert people building homes in flood zones that they do so at their own risk and will not be eligible for government relief if they suffer damage from high tides.

Interestingly, after the flooding in March 2014, I learned from talking to government officials in Majuro that to that point, there had been no flood zone mapping or surveying in the downtown area that is the most affected by floods. While it's probably true that atoll countries don't need new scientific data to tell them they should worry about rising sea levels, islands do need to conduct their own research to inform domestic government policies. In addition to the need to document at-risk flood zones in Majuro, the government could engage researchers to focus on coastal erosion trends, with the goal of informing government policy. Why this is important has been demonstrated by atoll research in the Marshall Islands by Dr. Murray Ford of the University of Auckland. A comparison of aerial photographs from the 1940s with today showed that Wotje Atoll, for example, had increased in size (an observation that runs counter to the usual claims about islands disappearing). But, he adds, a shift toward erosion could be occurring, underscoring the need for ongoing research to determine the status of shorelines around the Marshall Islands. "I've seen some sections of islands erode over a hundred feet, yet other nearby sections are completely stable," he said. "Any adaptation interventions need sound scientific data to support them."

Whether it's addressing regular inundation events or looking at longer-term erosion trends, Pacific islands need to do their homework — in the form of studies and surveys — so government decision makers have relevant information on which to base decisions. As the cost of emergency responses rises, this will be an increasingly critical need for small islands focusing on mitigation and building resilience.

While meetings multiply, climate action lags behind

It is remarkable that in light of known weather patterns in the Marshalls — January to April is the dry season — more long-term solutions for fresh water availability have not been implemented.

The remarkable thing about climate change in the Pacific is this: if meetings and conferences were an indication of action, then the islands should be winning the battle. Instead, pledges of billions of dollars for climate "resilience" and "mitigation" remain largely a mirage, while the big polluters that have caused the climate crisis continue business as usual. Occasional promises to reduce carbon emissions invariably gets derailed by political vagaries — or elections, such as the governments in Australia and New Zealand that have beat a retreat from climate action of earlier governments.

Some things are happening, of course, but they tend to be exceptions to the rule.

In mid-2014, the Federated States of Micronesia was in the news for adopting what is being touted as the Pacific region's first domestic climate legislation. The FSM's recently passed legislation requires the national and state governments offices responsible for the environment, disaster management, transportation, infrastructure, health, education and finance to mainstream climate adaptation in all policies and action plans.

Other countries in the region are in the early stages of drafting climate-specific legislation. Palau officials told me that as of June 2014, legislation was being drafted. In the Marshalls there is no legislation under development, but parliament Speaker Donald Capelle attended the World Summit of Legislators in Mexico, which was focused on looking at climate-related laws and rules — specifically, what is the role of national legislation in a post-2020 climate change agreement? Parliament officials in Majuro say they are hopeful of developing national legislation in the near future.

There is a draft bill before the Cabinet in the Marshall Islands for the establishment of a new Ministry for Climate Change, Environment, Energy and Conservation — which would consolidate all climate and energy offices under one roof, but has been under discussion now for over two years without being introduced to the parliament.

We regularly read about donor funds being available for projects aimed at boosting climate resilience and mitigation, but little money seems to actually be flowing into the islands. The Marshall Islands, like neighboring atoll nations Kiribati and Tuvalu, can legitimately lay claim to being on the front line of climate and sea level rise effects.

High tide events since 2008 (though there have been others prior to this) have caused significant and repeated damage to homes and businesses and government facilities on the ocean side of Majuro and other atolls in the country. Extended dry periods have also taken their toll, prompting aid agencies to respond with emergency and long-term assistance. Despite a seeming increase in flooding incidents, as well as ongoing coastal erosion that is destroying shoreline cemeteries, knocking down coconut trees, and causing hazards for housing built close to the high tide mark, there has yet to be a single government-sponsored "climate" response, such as shoreline revetment or seawalls in the lowest areas prone to constant flooding. Nor is any attempt made at urban zoning, with landowners given, by default, authority for allowing homes of any type, from shacks to concrete block buildings, to be built on even the most tenuous of coastal outcroppings.

In fact, the only significant climate funding into 2014 — other than funding for workshops and travel to get to workshops — has been a grant from the Secretariat of the Pacific Community/United Nations Development Program-managed Pacific Adaptation to Climate Change project with funds from the Global Environment Facility as well as Australia and the United States. This provided funding to re-line fresh water reservoirs in Majuro and provide covers to reduce loss of rainwater, which provides 95 percent of the fresh water on the atoll. A second element of the same grant is providing solar pumps and panels to outer island dispensaries that will be used to convert groundwater into safe drinking water.

It is also remarkable that in light of known weather patterns in the Marshalls — January to April is the dry season — more long-term solutions for fresh water availability have not been implemented. Instead, when an extended dry period hit the northern islands in 2013, donor agencies rushed bottles of water and small reverse osmosis water makers to these islands. Yet Utrik Atoll, in the northern Marshall Islands, has had a functioning solar and wind-powered large reverse osmosis water-making system in operation for nearly four years. Utrik is alone among northern islands in the Marshalls: when the rains stop four-to-six months of the year, Utrik has adequate potable water because of the large water-making unit.

Yet this system has not been cloned for other islands, which continue to suffer from extended dry periods that are exacerbated when the El Niño weather phenomenon develops.

Most small islands have little capacity to coordinate multiple donor projects, let alone navigate the labyrinth of donor applications and reporting requirements. And indeed a paradox of small islands is how bureaucracies defeat coordination among government offices. In the Marshalls recently, one government staffer posted a comment on Facebook critical of other government offices for traveling to multiple climate and energy conferences when they are not involved in domestic implementation. The point: there is a big disconnect between people traveling to climate meetings and action on the home front.

Very possibly the disconnect is the result of government people being more focused on attending the next climate meeting than they are on developing and implementing work at the community level that will make the legislation and the meetings meaningful to people at the grassroots.

Do Pacific islands need to 'walk the talk' on climate?

Governments in the region with trust funds have not addressed the apparent conflict between profiting from the oil industry and demanding it be phased down.

In late May 2014, a team of Greenpeace activists, including one from the Pacific, climbed aboard an oil drilling rig in the Barents Sea to protest offshore drilling, its contribution to climate damaging carbon emissions and the dangers of oil spills. Five months later, several dozen Pacific island "climate warriors" joined Australian colleagues in Newcastle for a daylong blockade of vessels carrying shipments of coal for export. The two protests were for the same purpose — to focus global attention on fossil fuels' contribution to climate problems — but with one significant anomaly: the oil rig targeted by Greenpeace was flagged in the Marshall Islands, one of several atoll nations at the forefront of an international campaign to cut back use of fossil fuels and reduce carbon emissions.

This raises the question: Do small island nations that contribute little to the carbon problem globally need to change their ways as they are demanding of big nations? More specifically, is it hypocritical for an island nation to demand reductions in use of fossil fuel while at the same time profiting from business investments in fossil fuel?

Seven nations in the Pacific — the Marshall Islands, Kiribati, Tuvalu, Federated States of Micronesia, Palau, Tonga and Nauru — operate government trust funds with significant offshore investment. Generally these are a mix of fixed income (government bonds), real estate and stock market investments. Because investments in the fossil industry have produced some of the greatest profits in the history of stock markets in recent years (except from late 2014 to mid-2015 as oil prices declined), virtually all big funds have some investment in the fossil fuel industry. A number of island nations also operate ship registries, led by the Marshall Islands, which has the world's third largest registry behind Panama and Liberia. Significantly for the Marshall Islands, a major portion of the tonnage it flags is oil tankers and drilling rigs.

The Marshall Islands has been at the forefront of the climate action campaign with Foreign Minister Tony deBrum and, more recently, Kathy Jetnil-Kijiner making headlines globally calling for nations of the world to act to prevent a climate disaster already in progress. But governments in region with trust funds have not addressed the apparent conflict between profiting from the oil industry and demands that it be phased down.

While the Marshall Islands' government has been silent at home on the issue, its voice internationally has grown greatly during Minister deBrum's tenure in government since 2012. During 2014, however, the College of the Marshall Islands took up a campaign for divestment from the fossil fuel industry. The college has a small endowment fund of about a million dollars that is invested in the U.S. and global stock markets.

"We will be crafting a policy statement for the Board of Regents so that the College of the Marshall Islands Endowment Fund is not investing in fossil fuel companies," said then-President Carl Hacker in late 2014. "It is something we can do to contribute to the change that is desperately needed." Jetnil-Kijiner, an instructor at the College of the Marshall Islands, has been a force behind the divestment movement with the college community.

The Majuro-based college is already the country's leader in renewable energy, and is getting ready to purchase electric vehicles. Since 2012, the college has slashed $300,000 a year off its electricity bill by expanding use of solar and wind power. Like action to use renewable energy, divestment is an important area for action, Hacker said.

The college administration engaged its Student Body Association to get students, teachers and staff talking about climate issues during a "divestment week" series of events in late 2014. During the week, SBA members went from class to class educating their peers about divestment. The students wrote essays, drew posters and participated in a public forum on the topic. The public event was titled "CMI and Divestment — putting our money where our mouth is."

These events at the college underscored the thinking of students, faculty and administrators that even though the endowment fund of CMI is relatively small and divesting will not affect fossil fuel companies, the issue is about taking a stand on principle. The students' message: The college should not talk about climate change and then reap interest from its investments in fossil fuel companies that profit by producing and selling the one product that is the largest contributor to climate change — fossil fuels.

In response to the divestment campaign within the college, the college board of regents in December 2014 directed the administration to divest from fossil fuel companies within three years.

The divestment campaign at the college hasn't spread to national government investments and the ship registry. But at some point the government, indeed all governments concerned with climate problems, will be forced to address the contradiction in demanding reduced global reliance on fossil fuels while at the same time profiting from the fossil fuel industry.

Thanks to donor funding, many Pacific islands have installed solar equipment on far-flung islands, bringing electricity for the first time to thousands of islanders and reducing modest usage of fossil fuel for power. These Pacific island actions are largely symbolic in terms of global impact, but everything from use of renewable energy and fuel-guzzling vehicles to divestment — or not — from the fossil fuel industry sends a message to the world about small island states walking the climate talk.

So far, most atolls are winning the sea level rise battle

Why the disconnect between scientific research and Pacific leaders' statements about climate effects matters.

An increasing number of atoll studies are not supporting claims of Pacific island leaders that "islands are sinking." Scientific studies published in 2015 show, for example, that land area in Tuvalu's capital atoll of Funafuti grew seven percent over the past century despite significant sea level rise. Another study reported that 23 of 27 atoll islands across Kiribati, Tuvalu and the Federated States of Micronesia either increased in area or remained stable over recent decades.

Speaking about Kiribati, Canadian climatologist Simon Donner commented in the Scientific American: "Right now it is clear that no one needs to immediately wall in the islands or evacuate all the inhabitants. What the people of Kiribati and other low-lying countries need instead are well-thought-out, customized adaption plans and consistent international aid — not a breathless rush for a quick fix that makes the rest of the world feel good but obliges the island residents to play the part of helpless victim."

These same climate scientists who are conducting ongoing research in Tuvalu, Kiribati and the Marshall Islands acknowledge the documented fact of sea level rise in the Pacific, and the potential threat this poses. But they are making the point, as articulated by Donner, that "the politicized public discourse on climate change is less nuanced than the science of reef islands."

A recent report carried in a 2015 edition of Geology, the publication of the Geological Society of America, says Tuvalu has experienced "some of the highest rates of sea level rise over the past 60 years." At the same time, "no islands have been lost, the majority have enlarged, and there has been a 7.3 percent increase in net island area over the past century."

To gain international attention to climate concerns and motivate funding to respond to what is described as climate damage, political leaders from the Pacific are predicting dire consequences.

"The future viability of the Marshall Islands — and all island nations — is at stake," Marshall Islands Foreign Minister Tony deBrum told the global climate meeting in Peru in December 2014.

"It keeps me awake at night," said Tuvalu Prime Minister Enele Sopoaga in a recent interview. "Will we survive? Or will we disappear under the sea?"

Obviously, statements of island leaders at international meetings and the observations of recent scientific reports are at odds. Does it matter?

Comments Donner: "Exaggeration, whatever its impetus, inevitably invites backlash, which is bad because it can prevent the nation from getting the right kind of help."

Scientists studying these low-lying islands should be seen as allies, whose information can be used to focus attention on key areas of need. For example, the New Zealand and Australian scientists working in Tuvalu said their results "show that islands can persist on reefs under rates of sea level rise on the order of five millimeters per year." With sea level rates projected to double in the coming years, "it is unclear whether islands will continue to maintain their dynamic adjustment at these higher rates of change," they said. "The challenge for low-lying atoll nations is to develop flexible adaptation strategies that recognize the likely persistence of islands over the next century, recognize the different modes of island change, and accommodate the ongoing dynamism of island margins."

Developing precise information on atoll nations as these scientists are doing is needed to inform policy makers and local residents as people are inundated with discussion about — and, possibly, outside donor funding for — "adaptation" and "mitigation" in these islands.

In the 1990s and early 2000s, the Nuclear Claims Tribunal in the Marshall Islands hired internationally recognized scientists and medical doctors to advise it on such things as radiation exposure standards for nuclear test clean up programs and medical conditions deserving of compensation, while evaluating U.S. government scientific studies on the Marshall Islands. These scientists and doctors provided knowledge and advice that helped inform the nuclear compensation and claims process.

It seems this nuclear test-related model would be of significant benefit to islands in the region, by linking independent climate scientists with island governments so there is a connection between science and climate policies and actions of governments.

If we want to grab headlines, the "disappearing island" theme is good. But to find solutions to, for example, the increasing number of ocean inundations that are occurring requires well-thought out plans.

"The reality is that the next few decades for low-lying reef islands will be defined by an unsexy, expensive slog to adapt," wrote Donner in the Scientific American. "Success will not come from single land purchases or limited-term aid projects. It will come from years of trial and error and a long-term investment by the international community in implementing solutions tailored to specific locales." He comments that a World Bank-supported adaptation program in Kiribati took eight years of consultation, training, policy development and identifying priorities to finally produce a plan of action. And even then, when they rolled out sea walls for several locations, there were design faults that needed to be fixed. Donner's observation about Kiribati could equally apply to the rest of the Pacific: "Responding to climate change in a place like Kiribati requires a sustained commitment to building local scientific and engineering capacity and learning from mistakes."

It is excellent advice.

Chapter Six: Unhealthy populations limit development progress

Increasingly over-populated urban centers in Pacific islands have limited opportunities for education, healthcare, jobs and recreation, and only sporadic access to fresh island foods. This has produced sedentary populations dependent on store-bought food that have high rates of lifestyle illnesses. In 2015, the World Health Organization said nine of the ten "most obese" nations in the world were in the Pacific. Photo: Ben Chutaro.

Diabetes needs community 'ownership'

Risk factors in the Pacific are feeding a pipeline of potentially expensive-to-treat NCDs, but governments are already fiscally constrained in how much they can provide to the health system.

A non-communicable disease (NCD) epidemic — with diabetes at its epicenter — is raging in urban centers throughout the Pacific, causing much more damage than debilitating health problems alone — though these, including cataracts, kidney failure and amputations, are bad enough.

The economic impact is significant and growing. In nine of twelve Pacific nations, reported the World Bank in a 2012 study on the economic costs of NCDs, these diseases account for seventy percent of deaths. In the Marshall Islands, for example, ninety percent of all hospital inpatient visits are related to NCDs, principally diabetes. Ministries of health today are shelling out large amounts of money to treat patients suffering from NCDs. Then there is the harsh economic reality that thousands of adults are being hit with symptoms of diabetes and other NCDs in their thiries and forties, preventing them from working. Just when people should be in a productive period in their lives, NCDs attack and the symptoms or side effects of the medications people take result in countless hours lost on the job — or worse. Finally, once people get into the end stage of diabetes, it becomes a huge burden — physically, mentally and financially — on their families who must care for increasingly disabled members of their family.

The statistics for Pacific islands are sobering. The Pacific region tops the world obesity and diabetes charts. For example, seventy-five percent of people in American Samoa, Nauru, and Tokelau are obese by World Health Organization standards. Other islands also show large percentages of their populations obese, a risk factor for diabetes: Kiribati (fifty-one percent); Marshall Islands (forty-five percent) Islands; Pohnpei, Federated States of Micronesia (forty-three percent); Solomon Islands (thirty-three percent); and Fiji (thirty percent). Diabetes rates are shockingly high, ranging from fourteen percent in the Solomon Islands to forty-seven percent in American Samoa. For perspective, diabetes affects three-to-six percent of Australians.

The Secretariat for the Pacific Community (SPC) put together a remarkable document with the bland title, "NCD Statistics for the

Pacific Island Countries and Territories," that contains charts titled "Low Physical Activity," "Hypertension," "Obesity," and "Low Fruit and Vegetable Consumption." The information contained in the SPC report should scare national planners in any island nation. In the "High Risk of NCDs" graph, only three countries — Papua New Guinea, Samoa and the Solomon Islands — are under 50 percent, no doubt at least in part because large numbers of their populations still live in villages where urban inactivity and a diet heavy in imported processed foods has not yet taken over. The majority of islands surveyed by the SPC show sixty to eighty percent of their populations at risk for NCDs.

The extent of the problem motivated the World Bank, in 2012, to issue a report on the economic impact of the growing NCD crisis. In reporting the "large health, financial and economic costs on countries," the World Bank made the point that financial burden on island nations is putting huge financial pressure on governments that already fund largely socialized health systems. "Risk factors in the Pacific are feeding a pipeline of potentially expensive-to-treat NCDs, but governments are already fiscally constrained in how much more they can provide to the health system," the World Bank report commented.

This report, like many on the issue, observed that "many of the NCDs are avoidable — or their health and financial costs can at least be postponed — through good primary and secondary prevention. This will require a more coherent approach to health system financing, and health system operations more generally."

Which gets us to the point: How can Pacific islanders counteract the debilitating scourge of NCDs? To do so means changing behavior, always a difficult undertaking. Health departments everywhere tend to engage in "health education" that advises readers or listeners to eat a healthier diet and to get exercise. In most urban centers, however, there is little room for gardens to improve fresh food availability — or, as poverty worsens, neighbors steal garden produce as it ripens, a big disincentive to making the effort to plant and raise backyard crops. Economic hardship is an obvious driver of diabetes, since an increasing number of urban dwellers can't afford to buy the fruits and vegetables they are urged by health educators to eat.

But equally problematic is exercise. If you're a student or in your early twenties, there are usually — depending on the island — organized volleyball, basketball, rugby or soccer leagues that offer good opportunities for fitness. For people in their thirties and older, what sports programs are organized on an ongoing basis? Not many, which means individuals have to motivate themselves to walk or jog or find a gym where they can work out. The statistics tell us that few do. For one thing, if you want to walk or jog, in many urban centers in the region, you must be armed with rocks or sticks to ward off attacking dogs, and you have to beware of drunk drivers. This is not an environment conducive to encouraging people who are new to the exercise routine to get out and do something (as a person who has been a jogger since my teen years, and is motivated for exercise, I know how hard it is to get out on the road to exercise in Majuro).

What I see is an obvious disconnect between government policy (combat NCDs through diet and exercise) and government action. In the Marshall Islands, for example, for the past several years a plan for a new hospital has been a priority, with a couple of million dollars invested in architectural designs for what could be a US$50-70 million facility. The last thing Majuro needs is an expensive facility that it will not have the money to maintain. Despite the declaration by government of a national health emergency for NCDs in late 2012, there have been no new sports facilities developed in Majuro by the national government.* A question is, why not take some of the money that is designated for a new hospital and use it to create recreation areas with walking tracks and sports courts such as basketball or tennis in high-population communities in the capital? This would be a first step to making it possible for people to follow the advice of the health promotion department.

A community group on the overcrowded island of Ebeye has broken new ground in efforts to curb the level of NCDs and particularly diabetes. Known as the Kwajalein Diabetes Coalition, the group conducted a community survey to find out what people knew about preventing NCDs. They learned that people in their small island were concerned there was no safe and accessible area for exercising, that the high cost of imported fruits and vegetables prevented people from eating a healthy diet, about a negative stigma associated with having diabetes, such that some don't want to acknowledge they have the disease, and had a general lack of understanding about the causes of the illness.

These are not eye-opening discoveries, but they gave the Coalition a starting point. They've engaged with the Taiwan Technical Mission to provide assistance in gardening techniques and seedlings for establishing a nursery that they hope will be one step to improving availability of nutritious foods.

What the Coalition is doing to address the exercise problem is innovative. They have rented a conference room at the main hotel on Ebeye, and turned it into an exercise room with a variety of exercise equipment that is open to the public. A longer-term plan to build a walking path is moving ahead through a partnership with the power and telephone utility companies. They have teamed up to all contribute to building a seawall, which will protect the utility companies' property, and making a lighted walkway on top of it.

"Our *Diak Plan* sets the framework for Kwajalein Diabetes Coaltion to lead a community-wide effort that aims to systematically reduce the burden of diabetes on our island community," says Romeo Alfred, who heads the group. "Diak requires the involvement of everyone onboard a sailing canoe. Our community's involvement in this evolving process gives hope that this whole effort will create a notable change in the quality of life for people suffering from diabetes and their families within the Kwajalein Atoll community."

Without government and donor investment in recreation and sports infrastructure, few people in the 30-60 age group living in urban areas of the Pacific will get out to exercise. A great example of this is Palau, where the government spent around a million dollars to construct a six-lane, all-weather track field as part of hosting the 1998 Micronesian Games. In the many years since, the facility has been used day and night by hundreds of runners and walkers in the main city of Koror.

Like the Kwajalein Diabetes Coalition collaborating with local utility companies to produce funding to create a walking track, we need to develop creative community partnerships, get governments to invest in recreation areas that encourage urban residents to exercise, and focus on the details needed to afford urbanites an improved quality of life. In the long run, this will provide opportunities to reduce the financial burden on government health services to treat the symptoms of these modern diseases.

* The only national indoor gymnasium located in Majuro has been closed since 2011 when a portion of its roof collapsed for lack of maintenance. It remained closed in 2015.

What to do about the Pacific's high teen pregnancy rates?

If there is a crosscutting problem, teen pregnancy is it, negatively impacting most aspects of life, particularly for people living in urban centers in the Pacific, where poverty is rising.

In today's health conscious world, people are bombarded almost daily with news about health crises. Depending on the country in the region, we can find these headlines in the news: Non-communicable diseases (NCDs) at epidemic level, TB rates spiral up, HIV infections rising, drug and alcohol abuse fuels school drop outs, high birth rate causes urban over-crowding, poverty on the rise.

A news item that caught my attention was from the Fiji Times: "Pacific nations have some of the highest teenage pregnancy rates in the world." Most Pacific governments have limited health resources that in many cases are already stressed by curative services focused on treating the symptoms of preventable illnesses (end-stage diabetes, for example). So where should governments focus interventions in their myriad development challenges, most of which are urgent in nature?

While NCDs, HIV, TB and other communicable diseases are important, teen pregnancy deserves a greater effort everywhere it's a problem, which, according to the United Nations Population Fund (UNFPA), is most countries in the Pacific. If there is a crosscutting problem, teen pregnancy is it, negatively impacting most aspects of life and development progress, particularly for people living in urban centers in the Pacific, where poverty is rising. Teen pregnancy often results in girls dropping out of school, ending their educational progress and reducing future employment prospects. The babies become an economic burden on the family, since rarely is the mother or father employed or prepared to rear a child. This often results in neglect and malnutrition, which sets the stage for a repeat of the drop out cycle. Teen pregnancies are by their nature high-risk, often presenting complications for the mother, baby and health care workers, increasing costs and problems.

In view of the fact that teen pregnancy rates have been high in the Pacific for years, it is fair to say that this issue has not grabbed the attention of government health and development policy makers in the region. Yet imagine if island countries were successful in slashing their teen pregnancy rates such that the hundreds — or in large countries in the region, thousands — of girls stopped having early births, completed secondary school, and had the chance to continue on to university. The economic impact alone of more educated young women would be startling, to say nothing of improved health and social conditions for the mother and her future children.

In the United States, the teen pregnancy rate has been consistently dropping for many years and reached a low of 2.9 percent in 2013. Although the U.S. is not always a good comparison for the Pacific, a key factor for the decline in the U.S. is relevant for the Pacific. Asked by Time magazine to explain the continuing decline in teen births in the U.S., Bill Albert, the chief program officer of the National Campaign to Prevent Teen and Unplanned Pregnancy, said: "The short answer is that it is a combination of less sex and more contraception. Teenagers have a greater number of methods of contraceptives to choose from."

Contrast that with the recent comment of Fiji Minister of Health Dr. Neil Sharma expressing concern over low usage of contraceptives in his country. But Dr. Sharma's concern is applicable to the teen populations in most Pacific nations. "The high rates of teenage and unplanned pregnancies and low contraceptive prevalence rates reaffirm the need to re-examine the way sexual and reproductive health and rights information and services are delivered to young people in the Pacific," said Voice of Youth representative Paulini Turagabeci at the UNFPA's launch of its new global population report in Fiji in 2013.

The Marshall Islands has consistently had the highest teen pregnancy rate in the Pacific, one that has hovered between fifteen and twenty percent of all births for decades. Despite the presence of Youth to Youth in Health, an innovative non-governmental organization that provides consistent focus on adolescent health, the important area of teen pregnancy prevention has been under-resourced for years.

An advertisement in the April 4, 2014 edition of the Marshall Islands Journal suggests that, while this is not a new phenomenon, it has risen to a new level of concern among people focused on health and development issues. The advertisement sought a "technical support consultant" to produce a "Prevention of Adolescent Pregnancy Strategy."*

While I believe the Marshall Islands' overwhelming reliance on consultants has been detrimental to the country, the challenge of teen pregnancy in the country has been a policy area neglected by government for decades. The joint plan by the Ministry of Health, Youth to Youth in Health, and UNFPA to tackle teenage pregnancy from a policy point of view, by developing a national strategy, is a much needed and long-overdue action. Whether a consultant is needed for this job is a question best left for a separate commentary. What is hopeful is that the Marshall Islands, together with an international donor agency, is preparing to step up interventions on a development issue that affects education, health and economic progress. It is not happening a minute too soon.

* The draft Prevention of Adolescent Pregnancy Strategy for the Marshall Islands was completed at the end of 2014. Like many policy reports prepared for the Marshall Islands government, however, it languished for months without final endorsement by government. As of June 2015, it had still not been formally adopted.

Chapter Seven: Nuclear Test Legacy Lingers

The 60th anniversary of the Bravo hydrogen bomb test was commemorated in Majuro in 2014 with a parade. Detonated at Bikini Atoll on March 1, 1954, the 15-megaton Bravo was the largest hydrogen bomb ever tested by the United States. March 1 is now a national holiday in the Marshall Islands in honor of nuclear test victims and survivors who were exposed to Bravo test fallout. Photo: Isaac Marty.

Nuclear legacy festers unresolved in the Marshall Islands

The 19-page Special Rapporteur's report on the Marshall Islands, issued in September 2012, was groundbreaking because it offered one of the first independent evaluations of the nuclear test legacy in the Marshall Islands.

In its campaign to garner support for a proposed Majuro Declaration on Climate Leadership at the 2013 Pacific Islands Forum summit in Majuro, the Marshall Islands government has back-burnered its long-standing concerns about unmet compensation, medical care, and clean up needs stemming from the United States nuclear weapons testing program at Bikini and Enewetak. This doesn't mean there isn't an effort going into securing language on the nuclear issue in the closing communiqué that will be issued at the end of the Forum summit. But while the U.S. nuclear legacy remains an important outstanding problem in the U.S.-Marshall Islands relationship, it won't be a major item on the Forum's agenda.

In fact, every year since the Forum meeting in Papua New Guinea in 1995, the communiqué has contained a section recognizing the "special circumstances pertaining to the continued presence of radioactive contaminants in the Republic of the Marshall Islands," and calling "on the United States of America to live up to its full obligations on the provision of adequate compensation and commitment to its responsibility for the safe resettlement of displaced populations, including full restoration to economic productivity and human enjoyment of all affected areas."

The 2012 Forum communiqué, adopted in the Cook Islands, updated the sentiment of support from the region by including a sentence about the planned presentation of a United Nations Special Rapporteur's report to the UN Human Rights Council in Geneva the month after the August Forum Leaders' meeting.

The nineteen-page Special Rapporteur's report on the Marshall Islands, issued in September 2012, was groundbreaking because it offered one of the first independent evaluations of the nuclear test legacy in the Marshall Islands. Generally, commentary on the U.S. nuclear testing program takes either the U.S. government's view or is vehemently critical. The dispassionate appraisal by Special Rapporteur Calin Georgescu lends significant credibility to the report. In actuality, any independent review of the U.S. nuclear testing will be critical because of the U.S. government's actions in relocating at whim islanders who were its wards under the UN Trusteeship Agreement, exposing them to nuclear test fallout, covering up reports about fallout exposure, repeatedly re-exposing islanders to radioactive environments that American scientists declared safe, and declaring as "full and final" a compensation settlement that was negotiated in bad faith and is clearly inequitable when contrasted with the compensation system accorded American "Downwinders" who lived near the U.S. nuclear test site in Nevada.

Special Rapporteur Georgescu takes an even-handed approach in his report, commenting: "The nuclear testing and the experiments have left a legacy of distrust in the hearts and minds of the Marshallese. The deep fissure in the relationship between the two Governments presents significant challenges; nonetheless the opportunity for reconciliation and progress, for the benefit of all Marshallese, is there to be taken."

He listed several pages of recommended actions for the U.S. and Marshall Islands governments, and for United Nations agencies. Ironically, the Special Rapporteur's report represents the first effort by the UN to address nuclear testing problems in the Marshall Islands — nuclear testing that its own Trusteeship Council endorsed in 1954 and 1956, brushing aside petitions from Marshall Islanders calling, politely, for a halt to nuclear tests that had exposed thousands of Marshallese to radioactive fallout and health injuries, and resulted in forced evacuations of hundreds of islanders.

Key recommendations in the report call on the U.S. government to pay all of the Nuclear Claims Tribunal's compensation awards. To this day, Marshall Islands nuclear victims have not received one hundred percent of their compensation because the Tribunal ran out of U.S.-provided compensation funds, and most of the awardees have died in the interim. As well, the Tribunal made only token payments on the large monetary awards for four of the nuclear test-affected atolls that sought compensation for nuclear cleanups, loss of use of land, and hardship. The UN report also recommended a comprehensive independent radiological survey be conducted through the auspices of the United Nations, and urged development of a comprehensive national health strategy to address cancer and non-communicable diseases.

During the September 2013 Pacific Islands Forum, Marshall Islands officials hope to gain Forum leaders' endorsement of the UN

Special Rapporteur's report.*

In light of last year's Forum communiqué that made special mention of what was then a soon-to-be-released report, it shouldn't be difficult to gain approval for a sentence in the communiqué endorsing the report. Because of the heavy focus of government leaders on climate change action in the lead up to this week's Forum in Majuro, little has been done by the Marshall Islands in the year since the UN report was presented to the Human Rights Council. Officials in Majuro say that is expected to change as they look to engaging the United Nations system in response to various aspects of the nuclear legacy — as recommended by the Special Rapporteur. A Forum vote of support, in the form of a paragraph in the communiqué, will give the Marshall Islands further leverage internationally as it pursues, however haltingly, a resolution to the impact that twelve years and sixty-seven nuclear weapons tests caused in the Marshall Islands.

* The 2013 Pacific Islands Forum Communiqué included several paragraphs about the UN Special Rapporteur's report and the nUS nuclear test legacy in the Marshall Islands. The communiqué said, in part: "Leaders recalled that the Republic of the Marshall Islands was placed by the international community under the trusteeship of the United Nations administered by the United States of America, both of which therefore have ongoing obligations to encourage a final and just resolution for the Marshallese people. They (the leaders) welcomed the recommendations in the Special Rapporteur's report...Leaders support bilateral and multilateral action to assist the Republic of the Marshall Islands in its efforts to engage the United States towards a justified resolution to the US nuclear testing program..."

'Waiting for these people to die'

Despite the release of documents that prove that many more than four atolls were affected by radioactive fallout, U.S. government officialdom maintains the fiction of the four atolls.

With the exception of two public hearings in the U.S. Congress in the mid-2000s, a petition from the Marshall Islands seeking additional compensation for nuclear weapons testing damages has languished since 2001. The lack of a formal response from the U.S. Congress and the Obama Administration prompted a Congressman from New York State, Gary Ackerman, to comment angrily during a 2010 public hearing: The Marshall Islands "claim we owe (them) $2 billion and so what? We're going to just wait for these people to die, right? We've given cancer to them, taken away their property...They've put a value on it, and it seems to me that if we know that this is about dignity, then there has to be something besides 'good luck fellows' with whatever few years you might have left...You can't unscrew them is the point. But we do compensate people for wrongs that we've committed. I know we're doing some stuff, and I know we spent half a billion bucks pretending to do the right thing, but they deserve to be compensated. What we did was inhuman and unconscionable."

Why is it that over sixty years after the Bravo hydrogen bomb test at Bikini Atoll on March 1, 1954, the U.S. nuclear legacy continues to vex relations between the Marshall Islands and Washington? Bravo, at fifteen megatons, was America's largest hydrogen bomb test. A thousand times more powerful than the atom bomb that killed one hundred thousand people in Hiroshima, Bravo spewed radioactive fallout on unsuspecting Marshall Islanders, U.S. servicemen monitoring weather conditions on Rongerik Atoll, and Japanese fishermen who had the misfortune to be fishing near the Bikini test site.

From day one, the U.S. government covered up the actual fallout impact not only of the Bravo shot but of all six of the large bombs tested at Bikini in 1954. The cover up went like this:

- The massive dose of radioactive fallout delivered to Rongelap Islanders, and to a lesser extent to those living on Utrik and other islands was the result of an "unexpected wind shift."
- At fifteen megatons, Bravo was two-to-three times greater than the anticipated power of the explosion. The power of Bravo,

however, as shown in recently declassified documents, was known in advance.

• Only Rongelap and Utrik were exposed to Bravo (or any other) test fallout.

All of these statements have been proven false by the release of formerly secret and classified U.S. government documents. Most significantly is the fact that eighteen other inhabited atolls or single islands around the country were contaminated by a minimum of three and most by all six of the bombs tested in Operation Castle, which included Bravo, in 1954.

But the myth of only four "exposed" atolls (Bikini, Enewetak, Rongelap and Utrik) has shaped U.S. nuclear policy toward the Marshall Islands since 1954, limiting medical and scientific follow up, and compensation programs.

In 1982 and 1983, when U.S. State Department and Marshall Islands negotiators were working out the details of a nuclear compensation agreement to be included in the Compact of Free Association, Marshall Islands leaders had no access to classified U.S. government documents that showed the extent of the fallout exposure in their islands. With the U.S. withholding pertinent nuclear fallout data, Marshall Islands leaders signed off on a compensation agreement that was felt to be the best deal that they could achieve — but the US$150 million trust fund was a far cry from the billions of dollars in value of lawsuits pending in the U.S. court system in the early 1980s that U.S. government officials wanted to eliminate with the Compact's nuclear compensation provisions.

And eliminate it they did. Once the Compact was signed and ratified as U.S. law by the Congress, U.S. courts said they could no longer hear the nuclear damage claims because the Congress had approved a political settlement. This settlement included the establishment of a Nuclear Claims Tribunals whose mandate was to adjudicate all claims, both personal injury and land damage/cleanup/loss of use. Marshallese claimants were told by an American judge that the Congress had provided an alternative compensation mechanism — the Tribunal — and therefore U.S. Courts could not hear their claims.

Fast forward 25 years and here is the situation:

• The Tribunal awarded US$96.6 million for personal injuries, but had funds to pay only US$73.5 million.

• The Tribunal awarded US$2.3 billion to Bikini, Enewetak, Rongelap and Utrik for loss of use, hardship, and nuclear clean ups, but had funds to make only token payments to Bikini and Enewetak amounting to about US$3.9 million.

As the Tribunal's situation was proving — for lack of U.S. funding — to be unresponsive to compensation awards approved, the Bikini and Enewetak communities refiled their lawsuits in U.S. courts in 2006. These were subsequently dismissed by the U.S. Federal Claims Court in late 2007, and an appeals court upheld the ruling. The U.S. Supreme Court declined to hear the cases, so Marshall Islanders have no standing to bring further legal challenges in the U.S. courts, a development that takes pressure off the U.S. Congress to address the situation.

Yet outside groups have consistently called on the U.S. government to pay the awards of the Tribunal. This includes a detailed review of the compensation situation by Harvard Law students that resulted in the report, "Keeping the Promise: An evaluation of continuing U.S. obligations arising out of the U.S. nuclear testing program in the Marshall Islands," published in 2006, and the 2012 report by a United Nations Special Rapporteur for the UN Human Rights Council, which among many recommendations called on the U.S. government to pay off the awards issued by the Nuclear Claims Tribunal.

While American "Downwinders" — people living in Nevada, Utah and Arizona who were exposed to nuclear test fallout from U.S. nuclear tests at the Nevada Test Site — receive all of their compensation awards, the more than 2,000 Marshall Islanders who received awards from the Tribunal were not paid one hundred percent of their compensation because of lack of funding.

The so-called "changed circumstances" section of the compensation agreement in the Compact of Free Association allows the Marshall Islands to petition the U.S. Congress for additional compensation if it can demonstrate that after approval of the compensation agreement in the mid-1980s, circumstances changed so as to render the compensation provided "manifestly inadequate."

The Marshall Islands submitted just such a petition in 2000 and resubmitted it in 2001. Except for two U.S. Congress hearings held in Washington, D.C. in 2005, and a Bush Administration report stating the U.S. government was not legally required to pay additional compensation, there has been no other official response from the Congress.

Quite simply the U.S. Atomic Energy Commission report entitled, 'Radioactive Debris from Operation Castle — Islands of the Mid-Pacific,' issued on January 18, 1955 but not publicly released until May 1994, nearly forty years after it was issued, constitutes "changed circumstances." This report, on page thirty-eight, provides a list of twenty inhabited atolls and single islands that were exposed to radioactive fallout from most of the six tests in the Castle Series in 1954. It explodes the myth created by the U.S. only four atolls that has been perpetuated by the U.S. government since 1954. This document, like thousands of other secret U.S. reports on its nuclear testing in the Marshalls, was withheld from Marshall Islands negotiators when the compensation agreement was negotiated in 1982-1983. The U.S. State Department negotiated the compensation agreement in bad faith. If Marshall Islands leaders had access to the treasure trove of secret U.S. reports on fallout exposure, they would have sought and likely held out for considerably more than the US$150 million trust fund put on the table by the U.S., as well as expanding health care and environmental monitoring programs to additional islands.

I have detailed this, including reference to many formerly classified documents, in my recently published book, Don't Ever Whisper. But the ongoing disconnect is problematic for the Marshall Islands. Despite the release of documents that prove that many more than four atolls were affected by radioactive fallout, U.S. government officialdom maintains the fiction of the four atolls.

Moreover, a key issue that has never been properly studied and evaluated is the impact of long-term exposure to low-dose radiation of people living and eating food grown in fallout-contaminated islands. U.S. doctors and scientists who, from 1954-1998 studied Rongelap and Utrik islanders, zeroed in largely on thyroid problems, while discounting the impact of low-dose radiation and such concerns as miscarriages and stillbirths. Because these areas have not been adequately investigated, there is a lack of "evidence."

There are many areas of the U.S. nuclear legacy that need serious engagement. The UN Special Rapporteur, among many recommendations, said the Marshall Islands should, "Carry out an independent, comprehensive radiological survey of the entire territory and, in this regard, request relevant United Nations agencies to undertake a study similar to the one conducted by IAEA on testing sites in other countries." He also called on the U.S. to provide "full access" for the Marshall Islands to U.S. government information and records "regarding the environmental and human health ramifications of past and current United States military use of the islands, as well as full access to United States medical and other related records on the Marshallese..."

Yet, in 2013, many documents remain classified, which prevents the Marshall Islands from understanding the full ramifications of the sixty-seven nuclear weapons tests conducted at Bikini and Enewetak.*

What does the future hold? Unless the Marshall Islands takes up the challenge to gain U.S. Congress support for expanded compensation and medical programs with an organized and systematic campaign of action, there is little hope that the U.S. Congress will ever on its own resolve the U.S. government's nuclear test legacy that continues to be a black mark on the relationship between the two countries.

* In 2014, 56 years after the last nuclear test was conducted in the Marshall Islands, the U.S. government declassified some reports with information about nuclear test fallout from the final two test series in 1956 and 1958 — weapons test series that accounted for three-quarters of all tests conducted in the Marshall Islands. These were the first reports containing information about nuclear test fallout to be released by the U.S. government on these two series of nuclear tests.

At 60, the legacy of Bravo still reverberates in Marshall Islands

The Marshall Islands needs to take nuclear test advocacy to the next level.

March 1 is a national holiday in the Marshall Islands marking the day the Bravo hydrogen bomb was exploded at Bikini Atoll, spewing radioactive fallout on islands around the Marshall Islands. The 60th anniversary in 2014 was marked in Majuro and other locations around the world. For most Marshall Islanders, it was a time to reflect on the fact that the U.S. nuclear weapons test legacy has left numerous unresolved issues for their nation.

One of the most important outstanding issues is the U.S. Congress' lack of official response to a petition for more compensation and health care funding submitted over thirteen years ago to Washington by the Marshall Islands government. The point of the petition, which was submitted pursuant to provisions of the Compact of Free Association, is to get the U.S. government to pay the awards adjudicated by the Nuclear Claims Tribunal, which was established by the Compact. Tribunal awards for personal injuries and only four of the most seriously affected atolls are over US$2 billion. These have not been paid because U.S. funding provided under the 1983 agreement proved to be far short of the amount needed to satisfy awards made by the Tribunal during its period of operations from the early 1990s to the late 2000s. Demonstrating the inequity of the situation, American "Downwinders" exposed to U.S. nuclear testing at the Nevada Test Site are treated differently. When the U.S. Congress passed a nuclear compensation law for Downwinders (and others) in 1990, it appropriated $100 million. When that initial amount did not cover the ongoing number of awards issued by the U.S. Justice Department, what did the U.S. Congress do? It responded by appropriating additional compensation funds. The amount paid out to Downwinders and other Americans exposed to radioactivity under this legislation has now risen to over US$1.8 billion.

Further demonstrating the inequity of the situation is what we know about exposures of Americans to Nevada tests and doses received by Marshall Islanders from tests at Bikini and Enewetak. Of course, what we know from declassified U.S. government reports does not reflect the true exposure, since monitoring in the 1950s captured only certain types of radiation and accounted only for external doses received. Still, what we know from these U.S. documents is instructive. The lowest average exposure of Marshall Islanders — who are considered by the U.S. government to be "unexposed" — is higher than the highest average exposure of Downwinders. It isn't surprising that Marshallese were dosed with higher amounts given that the Bikini and Enewetak tests produced over 90 times the yield of the Nevada experiments. For obvious reasons, the U.S. didn't test its hydrogen bombs in the continental United States, just as France and Britain used the Pacific for their tests. But what is surprising is that the U.S. government to this day, despite its own now declassified reports confirming the widespread extent of fallout contamination, still only recognizes four atolls as exposed. In fact, many more than Bikini, Enewetak, Rongelap and Utrik were exposed to harmful radiation from some of the sixty-seven nuclear tests.

A United Nations Special Rapporteur, in a report to the UN Human Rights Council in late 2012, urged the U.S. government to pay the awards issued by the Tribunal. He made numerous other recommendations to address ongoing problems caused by the nuclear test legacy. It is an independent and dispassionate appraisal of the situation, which confirms that sixty years on, many issues remained unresolved. The Special Rapporteur found that: "The nuclear testing resulted in both immediate and continuing effects on the human rights of the Marshallese...The effects of radiation have been exacerbated by near-irreversible environmental contamination, leading to the loss of livelihoods and lands. Moreover, many people continue to experience indefinite displacement."

The U.S. government, however, maintains that the Compact's $150 million compensation fund was "full and final" and that no further compensation is needed or required — despite the fact that the U.S. government withheld from Marshall Islands Compact negotiators secret reports that showed the widespread extent of fallout contamination that was not limited to the four atolls. The U.S. continues to fund limited health care and medical programs for people affected by the testing, as well as conducting ongoing scientific research and monitoring. But much more must be done to address nuclear clean up, health care and environmental monitoring and study needs.

The Marshall Islands government needs to step up its engagement on the issue, because a decade-and-a-half after its compensation petition was submitted to the U.S. Congress, it is clear the U.S.

government has little interest in addressing these issues. What is needed to advance Marshall Islands interests on this important issue is for the government to establish by law a nuclear agency with the mandate to pursue independent radiation environmental and health studies, gather information and resources, and pursue nuclear compensation, clean up and health funding and programs. Such an office would give these problems the focus they deserve, lending official sanction to efforts to resolve the legacy of American nuclear testing in the Marshall Islands.

Thinking locally before acting globally

The absence of a coherent strategy for engaging the U.S. to address the unresolved problems its nuclear testing caused has made it easy for American government officials to ignore the matter.

American lawyers acting for the Marshall Islands filed lawsuits against nine nuclear powers in the International Court of Justice and against the United States government in U.S. federal court at the end of April 2014, surprising the world with the unprecedented legal effort to enforce the Nuclear Non-Proliferation Treaty (NPT). In the Marshall Islands, people were just as amazed as virtually no one knew the lawsuits were coming.

As the ground zero for sixty-seven U.S. nuclear tests, the Marshall Islands has the moral mandate like few other countries to bring these lawsuits aimed at enforcing the disarmament terms of the NPT. Also, like few places in the world, it continues to experience the impact of a nuclear legacy of forced resettlements and life in exile, health problems from contamination by weapons test fallout, and nuclear test damage to islands requiring extensive clean up.

It is this nuclear legacy that continues to haunt relations between the U.S. government and the government and people of the Marshall Islands. The meaning behind the lack of a U.S. Congressional response to the Marshall Islands' request that it take steps to pay the Nuclear Claims Tribunal's awards for land damage, clean ups, and personal injuries, and the U.S. executive branch's "we already provided full and final compensation" position was aptly summed up by New York Congressman Gary Ackerman in 2010, when he observed: "We're going to just wait for these people to die, right?"

The lawsuits against the nine nuclear nations — United States, United Kingdom, Israel, France, Russia, China, India, North Korea, and Pakistan — have produced major media coverage and an outpouring of support from anti-nuclear groups around the world. "Our people have suffered the catastrophic and irreparable damage of these weapons, and we vow to fight so that no one else on Earth will ever again experience these atrocities," Marshall Islands Foreign Minister Tony deBrum said in a statement announcing the lawsuits filed April 24, 2014.

In comments at the United Nations in New York shortly after the lawsuits were filed, Minister deBrum described the Marshall Islands struggle to become an independent nation and member of the United Nations. "We are now a free country, but we are saddled with a period of nuclear testing by the United States from 1946 to 1958," he said. "As small as we are, we have a story to tell, we have an experience to share, and we have the motivation to pursue it to its just and peaceful end."

Outsiders might think it's a paradox that a nation that has suffered in the extreme from nuclear weapons testing does not have anti-nuclear groups and, in fact, has never had anti-nuclear organizations of the type established in developed countries. In fact, Marshall Islanders are anti-nuclear by experience; they just don't express it in the western conventional way. With the exception of a group known as "ERUB" — an acronym of the four most affected atolls (Enewetak, Rongelap, Utrik and Bikini) that is also a Marshallese word that means "broken" or "damaged" — generally in the Marshall Islands people take on nuclear issues representing their home atoll.

Another factor limiting nuclear victim advocacy is the government-to-government settlement that was approved in the first Compact of Free Association with the U.S. and implemented in 1986. That settlement was seriously flawed, as declassified U.S. government documents have shown many more islands than the four included in the settlement were affected by nuclear test fallout. Nevertheless, it produced trust funds for these four atolls that continue providing a modest level of funding for quarterly compensation payments, employment of people by the local governments, and various development projects. As a consequence, in recent years, government leaders, senators, mayors, and local government officials have shifted their attention from addressing strategies for gaining additional nuclear compensation, health care and clean up funding from the U.S. to a focus on managing trust funds and other U.S.-provided support such as funding for agriculture projects or supplemental food programs.

Not surprisingly, the absence of a coherent strategy for engaging the U.S. to address the unresolved problems its nuclear testing caused has made it easy for American government officials to ignore the matter.

Minister deBrum underlined an important point when he observed that, "The people of the Marshall Islands suffer quietly from many of the effects of the testing." The lawsuits in the International Court of Justice and in U.S. federal court are putting the spotlight on the Marshall Islands and its nuclear history. But it is an open question whether the lawsuits — which specifically state they are not seeking compensation — will help do what nuclear test-affected Marshall Islanders want, which is for the U.S. government to pay the over US$2 billion awarded — but not paid for lack of funds — by the Nuclear Claims Tribunal, a body established by the Compact of Free Association to adjudicate all nuclear claims in the Marshall Islands. A United Nations Special Rapporteur in 2012 urged the United States to pay the Tribunal's awards as one step to resolving its unfinished legacy. His report stated: "The nuclear testing resulted in both immediate and continuing effects on the human rights of the Marshallese...The effects of radiation have been exacerbated by near-irreversible environmental contamination, leading to the loss of livelihoods and lands. Moreover, many people continue to experience indefinite displacement."

At the United Nations in 2014, Minister deBrum commented: "We are still in constant negotiations, arguments, discussions with the United States about some of the effects of that testing."

In actuality, there has been little engagement with the U.S. government on the matter dating back a number of years with the exception of requests for release of still-secret nuclear test era reports on the Marshall Islands. There has also been little consultation with nuclear-affected islands about the new NPT lawsuits.

The apparent lack of consultation domestically about the NPT lawsuit strategy reflects a larger challenge of national development for the Marshall Islands. While its economy remains heavily dependent on outside donor aid — about seventy percent of the country's revenue comes from U.S., Taiwan and other donor grants — the Marshall Islands has chafed under what the current administration sees as heavy-handed, colonial-era control by the U.S. government over decisions about use of U.S. funding for the Marshall Islands. This has strained relations between the Marshalls and its largest donor partner, reducing overall dialogue and engagement between leaders from the two countries. For example, President Loeak, through three-and-a-half-years of his four-year term (which started January 2012), had yet to make an official visit to Washington, D.C. Meanwhile, his administration has faced — and defeated — two votes of no confidence since being elected in 2012. Hospital services hit their nadir in 2014, coupled with an unfolding bribery scandal involving hospital contracts. This is now the subject of criminal prosecutions in the High Court, continuing where earlier prosecutions of grant funding theft left off in 2011 and 2012. Earlier in 2014, the President complained on the floor of parliament about poor performance of government workers. In a nutshell, the

Marshall Islands has myriad and challenging domestic and donor-related issues in need of successful engagement, action and leadership.

Can these lawsuits help Marshall Islands nuclear test victims gain the nuclear clean up, health care, and compensation they seek and deserve? The suits are generating global media coverage, and will continue to so. They offer a platform for leaders to bring visibility to the long-ignored U.S. nuclear test legacy in the Marshall Islands. Whether the NPT lawsuits will help revive domestic dialogue and strategy development among nuclear-affected islands, and lead to engagement with the U.S. government is the big question waiting for an answer. Engagement at home on nuclear (and other) issues is a needed first step if the Marshall Islands is to benefit from these unprecedented NPT lawsuits.

Chapter Eight: Out-Migration Picks Up Steam

The 2011 national census for the Marshall Islands showed that four thousand people had left the remote outer islands since the previous census in 1999, roughly a quarter of the outer islands population. Many people from the outer islands, as well as the two urban centers of Majuro and Ebeye, have migrated to the United States, with an estimated 30,000 Marshall Islanders now living there.

Is it possible to make out-migration from the Pacific a success?

Investment in front end preparation in education, health and life skills training would offer migrating islanders a better chance of success.

Scientists — and political leaders in the Pacific — are increasingly dire in their predictions about potential inundation of islands by rising seas in the foreseeable future. At the same time, we are being inundated by news about potential "climate refugees" seeking help from Australia and New Zealand in particular.

In 2009, when only a few people in the region were talking about climate migration, University of the South Pacific Professor Patrick Nunn said many Pacific islands were in danger of extinction from sea level rise and should seek relocation aid. "By 2100, I don't see how many islands will be habitable," said Nunn, a Fiji-based professor of oceanic geoscience and a leading climate researcher. For coral atolls such as the Marshall Islands, Kiribati, Tuvalu and the Maldives — most of which are barely a meter above sea level — habitation will be impossible toward the end of the century, he predicted. But, he pointed out, it is a mistake to perceive sea level rise as an "atoll issue" because low-lying coastal areas — such as Fiji's Rewa Delta — will be heavily impacted by rising sea levels. Nunn's urgent recommendation: "If relocation is to happen by 2050, then by 2020 a plan must be in place."

While Kiribati, Tuvalu and the Maldives have been making headlines with climate appeals for a while, and lately have been joined by the Marshall Islands, planning for migration isn't yet being done, in large part because most people, including leaders, don't want to accept that the climate battle is a lost cause. Over the past couple of years, however, these issues are being broached in a more systematic way. A recent international conference hosted by the Columbia University Center for Climate Change Law asked a series of questions, including: If a nation is under water, is it still a state? What becomes of its exclusive economic zone? What obligations do other nations have to take in the displaced populations, and what are these peoples' rights and legal status once they arrive?

Is international migration the only solution for atolls, and internal migration the solution for coastal residents of high islands in the

Pacific? What is the experience of islands with migration to date that could offer clues to confronting the impending climate crisis?

The Marshall Islands may have the most experience with forced internal migration in the Pacific, with multiple populations moved to accommodate United States nuclear weapons tests at Bikini and Enewetak and missile tests at Kwajalein. Those experiences, commented Marshall Islands Cabinet Minister Tony deBrum during a media conference at the 2013 Pacific Islands Forum in Majuro, are "like fingernails on a blackboard. Our forced relocations have made the Marshall Islands extremely suspicious of relocation."

One of the few planned and islander-driven relocation efforts happened in the 1990s when Bikinians made a serious effort to purchase property on the Hawaiian island of Maui as a relocation site for their population. But the plan fell flat when it ran into opposition from the Maui community, largely due to concerns about access to land and how the Bikinians would integrate with the local community.*

In recent times the Marshall Islands, Federated States of Micronesia and Palau have seen large segments of their populations migrate to the United States — by ones and twos and in small groups — using the visa-free access in the Compact of Free Association treaties with Washington. Recent studies indicate that one-third of the Marshalls and FSM populations now live in the U.S. or its Pacific territories of Guam and Saipan — with out-migration continuing at a steady pace. Over forty-nine thousand from the FSM and over twenty-two thousand from the Marshall Islands now live in the United States.

How are these migrants doing in the U.S.? A 2012 survey by Francis X. Hezel, SJ, and Michael J. Levin of Micronesians living in the U.S. and its Pacific territories indicates that, in general terms, those who've moved to the U.S. mainland are faring better than those living in Guam and Hawaii. In the mainland, the survey found, there were fewer homeless, Micronesians were less dependent on welfare and food stamps, and had higher household incomes than their cousins in Hawaii, Guam and Saipan. High crime rates are often attributed to FSM migrants, particularly in Guam and Hawaii, and the Hezel/Levin report documented that four hundred and thiry FSM people have been deported from the US and its territories for committing felonies. No similar survey has been conducted on Marshallese living in the U.S., but islanders face many of the same challenges including a significant number of deportations following felony crimes in the U.S.

Many Micronesians and Marshall Islanders living in the U.S.

moved because the educational and job opportunities available in America don't exist at home. Some return home or are deported, but the vast majority is putting down permanent roots, with their children becoming U.S. citizens by virtue of birth in the United States.

Of the large numbers of people migrating to the U.S. mainland, many have headed to Midwest locations where factory jobs are easily available. The Springdale, Arkansas Marshallese community is apparently the largest concentration of one group of islanders in the U.S., with estimates of as many as ten thousand Marshallese living in this Northwest Arkansas area — and thousands more in the nearby states of Missouri and Oklahoma.

The visa-free access provision in the Compacts was a trade for the defense control the United States maintains in these three U.S.-affiliated island groups. In the 1980s, when U.S. and island negotiators hammered out these treaties, they saw U.S. access as both a safety valve for small islands that had little opportunity to create job opportunities for their citizens as well as a means for islanders to gain education and experience that they could use back home. The safety valve has proved itself in light of stagnant economies in the FSM and Marshall Islands coupled with generally poor quality public schools. A reasonable number of Marshall Islanders who complete college education in the U.S. are returning home to work. But islanders' ability to gain work without need of special permits has resulted in extraordinarily high dropout rates from U.S. colleges. Low-performing public schools in the islands have not prepared most young people to compete in a U.S. academic environment, relegating many to entry level jobs with little hope for advancement.

"Relocation is one of the most difficult things to talk about and to convince people that the home they've lived in for centuries is no longer a viable option," said Nunn in addressing a future where sea level rise is a fact, not a prediction.

Perhaps the best advice that can be offered is that for islanders who are migrating to the United States and for those who may be forced by climate-caused sea level rise to move to Australia, New Zealand or other large countries in the future, preparation at home is a key first step to successful resettlement. Hezel and Levin make an interesting point about how Micronesians work to maintain their culture while living in the U.S.: "FSM migrants may have left their home islands, but they have not abandoned their language or culture. Most FSM people prefer to use their native language at home with their family, even if they must speak English most of the time in the school or the workplace. Women everywhere continue to wear the distinctive dresses that identify them as Micronesian."

But ability to speak English and appreciation of cultural and behavior norms in their new home is a good recipe for making a successful transition. Many Marshall Islanders and Micronesians have had to learn this the hard way through trial and error in a country whose legal system is not forgiving or prone to offering second chances. Addressing education and life skill requirements at home requires a level of planning and preparation that has not existed in either the FSM or the Marshalls and, in fact, seems like an improbable hope. Still, as people consider the possibility of the need for eventual climate-driven migration, all countries that have relations with these small Pacific islands would do well to invest in front end preparation in education, healthcare and life skills training that would offer out-migration a better chance of success.

*In March 2015, the Mayor of Bikini, Nishma Jamore, announced that the Bikinians living on Kili and Ejit Islands wanted to migrate to the U.S. Increasingly bad flooding from high tides and storms at both islands prompted Bikini leaders to bring up the concern with U.S. government representatives.

Are migration challenges faced by islanders and U.S. states fixable?

Mounting problems facing American states and territories attempting to meet needs of in-bound islanders need high-level engagement and action.

Out-migration to the United States of tens of thousands of islanders from U.S.-affiliated islands has become a front-burner issue for U.S. states and territories hosting the largest numbers, with headlines — mostly negative — now regularly in the media. Hawaii and Guam, in particular, are raising the volume of their complaints to the U.S. federal government over lack of reimbursement for health and education costs, and other areas — Arkansas, for example, where thousands of Marshall Islanders live — are likely to follow.

Since 1986 when the first Compact of Free Association came into effect between Washington and the Federated States of Micronesia, Marshall Islands and Palau, citizens of these three freely associated states (FAS) have had visa-free access to the U.S. to study, work and live.

The tempo of out-migration picked up in the mid- and late-1990s, particularly from the FSM and Marshall Islands, as job markets remained stagnant, and health and education services declined.

When Guam Governor Eddie Calvo said at a Washington, D.C. meeting of governors in February 2015 that FAS citizens were pushing Guam government agencies "to the breaking point," and said the problem was many in-bound FAS migrants were uneducated and unhealthy, it ratcheted up official state concern about migration to a new level. This follows the state of Hawaii's decision reached in late 2014, supported by U.S. courts, to stop providing expensive dialysis and cancer treatment to most FAS citizens as of March 1, 2015.

Recent estimates suggest the number of FAS citizens now in the U.S. is approaching one hundred thousand, though more and more are American citizens by virtue of birth in the U.S. The large numbers in Hawaii, Guam, Arkansas, Oregon and Washington, to name a few, are beginning to stand out with state agencies under budget pressure as they attempt to provide health and social services with dwindling resources.

Although officials from the FAS often attend meetings to discuss what is called "Compact impact," there has been little engagement overall with these far-flung communities.

Noted Micronesia commentator Fr. Francis X. Hezel observed recently: "Some who have chosen to remain in the islands may think of the migrants as people who have deserted their homeland when things became tough. Sometimes political figures in FSM can put their own stamp on this position, as when they state that migrants have made their choice to leave and so should be left to take care of themselves without any help from FSM government. At times, political leaders seem to regard migrants as an embarrassment on the grounds that they bring unwelcome attention upon FSM. There are, of course, abundant stories of people getting tossed into jail, or filing for federal benefits within hours after they have landed. But the real problem for those FSM leaders may be that the very number of people leaving seems to be evidence that the problems back home haven't been fixed: lack of jobs in a struggling economy, a mediocre educational system, and the absence of the advanced health care that many require."

The fact that these islands have some of the highest rates in the world of tuberculosis, Hansen's disease and diabetes tends to complicate the situation of FAS migrants in the eyes of officials providing services in U.S. areas.

What can and should be done to deal with both the legitimate budget concerns of areas such as Guam and Hawaii, and the legitimate needs of a group of people who are legally in the United States pursuant to treaty from which the U.S. government derives numerous benefits? One major problem is that a U.S. law adopted in 1996 removed Medicaid health coverage for FAS citizens, which has put islanders at the mercy of state-level health care. Since a large number are uninsured and ineligible for federal or state health insurance programs, FAS citizens tend not to seek early health care because of costs. So many end up in emergency care situations, increasing hospital costs exponentially.

A paper published in the American Journal of Public Health in early 2015, "Effect of U.S. policies on Health on Health Care Access for Marshallese Migrants," argues that U.S. federal and state health policies should be changed to extend health care coverage to citizens of the Marshall Islands and other freely associated states legally living in the U.S. and its territories. "Marshallese persons and all Compact of Free Association (COFA) migrants in the United States (should be) treated as equal and have access to affordable, quality health care." Given that health benefits have been incrementally restored for most other legal immigrants in the U.S.

since the U.S. Congress cut off Medicaid in 1996, it is hardly an unreasonable recommendation.

An important point made by this paper written by three U.S. university-based Americans is this: "Securing health care coverage for Marshallese migrant children is an important part of improving the overall health of the Marshallese community." This observation equally applies on the home front in the FSM and Marshall Islands, which have been unable to get a grip on communicable and non-communicable diseases that are spiraling out of control. Greater focus on improving the health of citizens resident in the FSM and Marshall Islands would have a positive impact on how arriving FAS immigrants are perceived in the United States, as well as reducing costs.

There is no question FAS countries are benefitting from the migration opportunity provided by the Compact of Free Association. With few job opportunities and stressed education and health systems, what would the FSM and Marshall Islands do if the nearly one hundred thousand islanders now resident in the U.S. were still living at home? In addition, with thousands of FAS citizens now employed in the U.S., albeit largely in entry-level positions, it is resulting in remittances to families back home, which is a huge benefit as economic conditions in the islands have shown little improvement in recent years. FAS citizens also fill a gap in Guam and U.S. states: they are filling entry-level and factory jobs that many U.S. citizens don't want. In addition, hundreds of islanders enlist in the U.S. military at a higher per capita rate than Americans, the U.S. military has control of a western Pacific ocean area nearly the size of the continental U.S., and the Reagan Test Site in the Marshall Islands is a key part of the Defense Department's missile defense program.

One state-level intervention shows a model for successful engagement by U.S.-resident FAS citizens. The Oregon state-based CANN — the Compact of Free Association (COFA) Alliance National Network — engaged state legislators and the governor two years ago to gain passage of a law making FAS citizens eligible for the same state identification and driver's licenses as other Oregon residents. A 2005 federal law blocked issuance of all but temporary ID to FAS citizens, negatively affecting their ability to get jobs and housing. CANN has now gained support from legislators for the introduction of legislation to provide health care to FAS citizens living in Oregon. Though the bill may face challenges, since it was introduced at the end of January 2015, it has gained support in the media and from American military veterans, among others.

Clearly legislation and policy action at the national level would help needs of FAS citizens living in the U.S. and is preferable than mounting multiple state-level efforts. The Oregon model suggests that active engagement with media, the community, and legislators has a positive outcome. Generally, this type of engagement by FAS government or community leaders in relation to Guam and Hawaii has been lacking except as a reaction to negative publicity or budget cutting moves, such as Hawaii has now taken to cut its spending on health care services for FAS citizens.

Relative to citizens of other nations attempting to migrate to the U.S., the estimated one hundred thousand FAS citizens in the United States are barely a blip on the radar and would remain so even if the entire populations of the FSM and Marshall Islands, roughly one hundred and sixty thousand, moved to America tomorrow. In many states, they are small minority, though not so in smaller places like Guam and Hawaii.

Since both the U.S. federal government and the FAS governments benefit from the provisions of the Compact, positive action on these issues is called for. Moreover, it offers the FAS governments more than some positive public relations to engage at the federal and state level for their citizens in America — it offers a platform for addressing other issues of concern within the free association relationship. The Oregon results suggest the benefits of engagement with legislators.

Suggestions for Further Reading

• Making Sense of Micronesia: The Logic of Pacific Island Culture, Francis X. Hezel, University of Hawaii Press, 2013.
• Don't Ever Whisper: Darlene Keju — Pacific Health Pioneer, Champion for Nuclear Survivors, Giff Johnson, CreateSpace, 2013.
• Nuclear Past, Unclear Future, Giff Johnson, Micronitor, 2009.
• Flight of the Dudek: A Story of One Person's Journey, Paul Callaghan, CreateSpace, 2012.
• Surviving Paradise: One Year on a Disappearing Island, Peter Rudiak-Gould, Union Square Press, 2009.
• For the Good of Mankind: A History of the People of Bikini and their Islands, Jack Niedenthal, Micronitor, 2001.
• Bravo for the Marshallese: Regaining Control in a Post-Nuclear, Post-Colonial World, Holly M. Barker, Cengage Learning, 2012.
• The Consequential Damages of Nuclear War: The Rongelap Report, Barbara Rose Johnston and Holly M. Barker, Left Coast Press, 2008.
• Operation Crossroads: The Atomic Tests at Bikini Atoll, Jonathan M. Weisgall, Naval Institute Press, 1994.
• Report of the Special Rapporteur on the implications for human rights of the environmentally sound management and disposal of hazardous substances and wastes, Calin Georgescu, United Nations Human Rights Council, 2012.

Websites and blogs

• Comment and analysis on Micronesia by Fr. Francis X. Hezel, S.J.: http://www.wheresfran.org/
• Pacific Institute for Public Policy: www.pacificpolicy.org/
• Parties to the Nauru Agreement: www.pnatuna.com/
• Graduate School USA, Pacific and Virgin Islands Training Initiative, with economic and performance reports on the FSM, Palau and the Marshall Islands: http://www.pitiviti.org
• Commentary and original poetry on climate, racial discrimation, writing, and other contemporary island issues by Kathy Jetnil-Kijiner: https://jkijiner.wordpress.com
• Auckland University of Technology Pacific Media Center: www.pmc.aut.ac.nz
• What we know about Climate, American Association for the Advancement of Science: http://whatweknow.aaas.org

Made in the USA
Middletown, DE
15 July 2015